# The Summons of the Text

# The Summons of the Text

*How Every Text Points to the Gospel*

BRUCE G. GALE

*Foreword by* Matthew F. McKellar

WIPF & STOCK · Eugene, Oregon

THE SUMMONS OF THE TEXT
How Every Text Points to the Gospel



Wipf & Stock
An Imprint of Wipf and Stock Publishers
199 W. 8th Ave., Suite 3
Eugene, OR 97401

www.wipfandstock.com

PAPERBACK ISBN: 979-8-3852-6685-2
HARDCOVER ISBN: 979-8-3852-6686-9
EBOOK ISBN: 979-8-3852-6687-6

To Shannon, Caleb, Elias, and Joshua—
you are my daily reminders that legacy is not written on pages but formed in the character we model, the faithfulness when no one is looking, and the faith we impart. You make me want to be a better man and are my richest blessing from the Lord.

# Contents

# Foreword

During my days as a doctoral student, I recall taking a course entitled Seminar in Persuasion. The major premise communicated in it was that one of the primary objectives of most verbal communication was to persuade. Unfortunately, the very concept of persuasion has fallen on hard times in recent years, particularly among those charged with the task of proclaiming God's word to their generation. Not infrequently, voices arise which equate all efforts at persuasion as equal to attempts to coerce or manipulate. Yet, from a Christian perspective, while rejecting manipulative or coercive communication, the Scriptures clearly support the concept of compassionate persuasion.

Writing to the gifted but problematic church at Corinth, the apostle Paul wrote, "Therefore, knowing the fear of the Lord, we persuade people" (2 Cor 5:11). Using a participial form of the verb *peitho*, Paul unapologetically connects the validity of attempts to influence or persuade the thoughts and actions of hearers to a healthy and foundational reverence or awe of the living God. Paul's Spirit-inspired writings and Spirit-driven missionary activities profoundly indicate that his objective in sharing the gospel of Jesus Christ extended far beyond the mere transmission of information.

Of course, a resolute commitment to the accurate transmission of biblical truth is both desirable and necessary for faithful preachers. Such a commitment is reflected in the text-driven philosophy of preaching which stresses that the biblical text must govern the substance, structure, and spirit of a sermon. Today's true expositors owe a debt of gratitude to text-driven trailblazers like David Allen and Steven Smith. These men, and others, blazed a trail of recommitment to the matter of "letting the text talk" in every sermon.

However, at the same time, a host of text-driven preachers would advocate vehemently that the transmission of truth is connected vitally to the worthy goal of life transformation. The very nature and testimony of written revelation reflect this objective. The creation account in Genesis points us to a God who calls a world into existence out of nothing. He calls and an ordered cosmos is fashioned, testifying to his glorious handwork. Later in the Old Testament we observe God's initiative in calling Abraham and, after that, prophets like Isaiah and Jeremiah. In the pages of the New Testament the Gospel writers record the arrival of the incarnate Son of God. The Lord Jesus Christ communicates truth about himself and his Father. Yet, in the context of that communication we find him calling crowds to hear with intent to obey and disciples to follow him decisively and without delay.

The author of the book you hold writes, and correctly so, with the conviction that the gospel message by its very nature calls for response. His contention is that this "call" should receive greater emphasis in the processes of sermon preparation and delivery. Therefore, with a lucid style and a core commitment to biblical authority and sufficiency, Bruce Gale makes a reasonable and riveting appeal for the inclusion of the biblical text's summons, its invitation or call to response, as a defining element of text-driven preaching, along with the elements of substance, structure, and spirit.

Gale's argument for the addition of the "summons" to the current threefold rubric of text-driven preaching is made on biblical, theological, and historical grounds. His "golden chain of evangelism," referenced in the fifth chapter, is particularly insightful, as it skillfully weds sermonic content with sermonic call. Ultimately, viewing the summons as a vital element in faithful biblical proclamation, his advocacy for honoring the truth of the text as well as its intent to transform is a compelling case for the inclusion of the "summons" in the text-driven model.

Finally, on a personal note, I am delighted to recommend this book written by my gifted former student and forever friend. His passions for gospel truth and gospel transformation flow consistently out of his pen and his personal life. I gladly join with him in the inestimable privilege of summoning this generation to the beauty and worth of King Jesus!

Matthew McKellar
Professor of Preaching, George W. Truett Chair of Ministry
Southwestern Baptist Theological Seminary
Fort Worth, Texas
February 2026

# Introduction

In an age marked by shifting cultural convictions and evolving ecclesiastical methodologies, the proclamation of Scripture remains central to the life and mission of the church. Among the various homiletical frameworks, the threefold text-driven preaching model has emerged as a compelling structure for faithful engagement with the biblical text. Yet, a lingering question challenges its completeness: Should this model intentionally incorporate the text's summons—the moment where Scripture not only informs but calls, convicts, and commissions?

This book was born out of that very inquiry. Drawing upon historical, theological, and qualitative research methods, it endeavors to assess how and to what extent the summons of the text—commonly expressed as the invitation or call to response—should be included as a defining element in text-driven preaching.

Through the evolution of preaching, the meaning of expository preaching has become suspect in its uses. The confusion lies in the fact that there are extremes who call themselves expository preachers. One example is when preachers read a section of text in the introduction and then launch into a diatribe of their own thoughts. Another error is when the preacher exegetes a text from the pulpit and calls it expository. Still another takes a passage and preaches a theme that may or may not be the author's intended message and calls it expository. Moreover, pastoral commentaries on social woes have often been passed off as exposition. David Allen stepped in and rose to the challenge, offering text-driven preaching to clarify the conversation. The text-driven preaching hermeneutic seeks, as its chief aim, the truth that God has spoken.[1] Furthermore, Adam Hughes stated, "The expository sermon is founded on direct biblical authority and driven

1. See David L. Allen, introduction to Akin et al., *Text-Driven Preaching*, 3.

by what is taken out of the text directly and precisely."[2] The essential idea of text-driven preaching is that sermons should be based upon a particular text of Scripture and expound its meaning.[3]

What lies at the heart and soul of text-driven preaching? This book seeks to explore the richness of the theology that supports text-driven preaching, as well as the foundational model that comes from this theological conviction—the substance, structure, and spirit of the text. Preaching is the ministry of the word of God to the people toward the end of salvation and sanctification.

In addition, it seeks to define the summons of the text and provide a high-level argument for its inclusion in sermon preparation. This looks to clarify the distinction between the summons and the application of the sermon, the biblical and theological implications, the philosophical and pedagogical necessity, and finally the practical application of the summons. A part of that aim is to establish the biblical evidence for the ubiquity of Christ throughout Scripture. This understanding demonstrates the necessity of seeing the revelation of Christ and of calling for a response to it in the text.

Moreover, it demonstrates the apostolic *kerygma* and its use of the Old Testament to proclaim the risen Lord Jesus. This explains the Christocentric theology of preaching that undergirds expository preaching. An understanding of the apostolic kerygma establishes the New Testament precedent for the summons and is therefore vitally important. This book offers a biblical foundation looking to Peter and Paul to demonstrate dependence upon the summons. And it establishes what I am calling the "gospel chain of evangelism." Looking at Rom 10 reflects the necessity of the culmination of the gospel proclamation that flows from Christ and then returns glory to Christ. The declaration of the gospel message of Jesus demands both a preacher and a response because the gospel begins and ends in him.

Then, the gospel message within the word of God should permeate the whole of ministry, especially the pulpit ministry. This preaching principle aligns with Paul's declaration in 1 Timothy. Paul's appeal to the preaching of the word demonstrates the impact of rhetorical persuasion on the hearer. This stands as the crux of the theological argument for the inclusion of the summons appealing to the mind, emotions, and volition.

2. See Adam Hughes, "The Soul of the Evangelistic Expository Sermon," in Price, *Engage*, 449.

3. See David L. Allen, introduction to Akin et al., *Text-Driven Preaching*, 7.

The notion of the summons is rooted in the conviction that the goal of any argument in an expositional sermon should be to persuade the hearer toward a deeper understanding of and dependence upon Christ. Sermons, since the dawn of preaching, employed persuasion to communicate the truths of God from Scripture. Persuasion in expository preaching rests on a twofold dichotomy: reliance upon the Holy Spirit and expounding the text itself. The persuasive nature of rhetorical functions is subordinate to the meaning and message of the text of Scripture.

Furthermore, this book demonstrates that the gospel is the culmination of God's revelation of himself to mankind. Therefore, there is an inherent expectation of response from that proclamation. God reveals his divine character and attributes through Scripture. In light of that revelation, man must respond. The text calls for a change in mind, emotions, and will. Six textual examples of encountering God are provided, with the bonus of examining the substance, structure, spirit, and summons of each passage.

This book unifies the argument that the power of the gospel must infiltrate the innermost affections of the heart, permeate the soul, and compel the hearer to respond.[4] The summons must align with a more excellent canonical view to ensure biblical consistency with the whole of Scripture. Therefore, the conviction of the centrality of the gospel in preaching must be unmistakable. Paul commended preaching the word—the message of Christ—and in preaching, the word must reprove, rebuke, and exhort.

4. Calvin, *Christian Life*, 13–14.

# CHAPTER 1

# Why Text-Driven Preaching

By the time I had heard of text-driven preaching, I had read several "how-to" expository preaching books. None of them was bad per se, but the one thing they had in common was that they were all practical. I do not know about you, but the way my brain is wired, I need to know the "why" behind the "how" before I can really grasp the content. Then I read the book *Text-Driven Preaching*. Why was this book so different? Because, although it was practical in its own way, it addressed the convictional "why." Text-driven preaching, like all approaches to faithful exposition, stands upon biblical authority as its center. The sufficiency of Scripture affirms that the word of God is enough. Greater than any gimmick tossed from the pulpit, the word of God transforms the whole man. The preacher stands confidently on the strength of Scripture and wholly depends on the Holy Spirit to communicate to the people. This confidence is why text-driven preaching is not a style but a theological and philosophical conviction. Text-driven preaching goes beyond verse-by-verse exposition. It strives to let the text shape the message from every facet of presentation. A text-driven preacher does not preach sermons; he preaches texts. This chapter walks through a brief history of the development of text-driven preaching.

## The Development of Text-Driven Preaching

Confusion has mired our current understanding and definition of expository preaching. This confusion has resulted from pragmatism replacing conviction. All too often, we find that running commentaries passed off as exposition detract from clarity.[1] From this confusion, a need arose to clarify expositional preaching. In comes text-driven preaching, which seeks, as its chief aim, the truth that God has spoken.[2] Since God has spoken through his written word, it is imperative to base the dissemination of his word—the sermon—upon the text. Robby Gallaty and Steven Smith asserted, "Text-driven preaching is the interpretation and communication of a biblical text in a sermon that re-presents the substance, structure, and spirit of the text."[3]

### *Hermeneutical Foundations*

In 2010, David Allen laid the foundations of text-driven preaching in his seminal work as a contributing editor of *Text-Driven Preaching: God's Word at the Heart of Every Sermon*. He drew attention to the fact that many modern sermons profess to be expository but lack conviction in practice and exist only in name.[4] By his estimation, the issue rested in a lack of dependence upon the text of Scripture as "the biblical text becomes for many not the source of the sermon but merely a resource."[5] This lack of dependence upon the text reveals several false assumptions about sermons, often standing in stark contrast with expositional preaching. Allen attested that "on any given Sunday," there are a multitude of preaching styles in churches across the globe—creative, narrative, post-psychology, the new homiletic, and topical. However, there is a clear distinction between expository preaching and the rest.[6]

Ultimately, expository preaching stands in contrast to the aforementioned outworkings of experiential preaching. Upon this observation, preaching influenced by the New Homiletic—a subsequent by-product of the New Hermeneutic—strives to develop a sermon experience based upon a text of Scripture that is often to the detriment of the truths of Scripture. Allen asserted, "Sermons should not only be based upon a text of Scripture but should also actually expound the meaning of that text."[7]

1. Strain, *Expositional Preaching*, 45.
2. See David L. Allen, introduction to Akin et al., *Text-Driven Preaching*, 3.
3. Gallaty and Smith, *Preaching*, 25.
4. See David L. Allen, introduction to Akin et al., *Text-Driven Preaching*, 2.
5. See David L. Allen, introduction to Akin et al., *Text-Driven Preaching*, 7.
6. See David L. Allen, introduction to Akin et al., *Text-Driven Preaching*, 1.
7. See David L. Allen, introduction to Akin et al., *Text-Driven Preaching*, 5–6.

What is more, Allen illuminated the necessity for clarity. This clarity arose from infusing linguistics into the hermeneutical process of exegesis. His argument asserted that the text had meaning for its original audience and that this meaning is universally relevant and should be applied to congregations today. He contended, "Linguists now point out that meaning is structured beyond the sentence level."[8] Therefore, hermeneutics necessitates an analysis of the phonology, morphology, syntax, and semantics. That is to say, words make sentences, paragraphs, and complete thoughts. Meaning derives from these complete thoughts. This approach exemplifies linguistically capturing the passage's context.

The foundational influence of text-driven expository preaching rests firmly on God speaking. This theological position rests upon the work of Peter Adam, *Speaking God's Words: A Practical Theology of Preaching*. Allen asserted, "God is a God who speaks."[9] The distinction of expositional preaching anchors in the inspiration of Scripture—God's chosen means of communicating with his people. He further attested, "Expository preaching, therefore, emerges not only as a type of sermon but as a theological outgrowth of a high view of inspiration."[10] Where expositional preaching seeks to capture the text's central idea, text-driven preaching seeks to capture the text's central idea, its structure, and its feel, and then re-present the text's order and flow in the sermon.

## *Homiletical Form*

Moreover, Steven Smith provided homiletical meat to the hermeneutical skeletal bones of text-driven preaching. He applied the text-driven model—the substance, structure, and spirit—as the components of text-driven expository preaching. He argued, "Once the exegetical work is complete and we know what the text says, the temptation is to take the meaning of the text and present it in any homiletical form we like. . . . The shape of the sermon is not arbitrary. . . . The text-driven sermon is based on the substance, structure, and spirit of the text."[11] Text-driven expositional preaching is a

8. See David L. Allen, introduction to Akin et al., *Text-Driven Preaching*, 6.

9. See David L. Allen, "Preparing a Text-Driven Sermon," in Akin et al., *Text-Driven Preaching*, 101.

10. See David L. Allen, "Preparing a Text-Driven Sermon," in Akin et al., *Text-Driven Preaching*, 103.

11. Smith, *Recapturing the Voice of God*, 19.

philosophical conviction, anchored in rich theology, rather than a stylistic preference.[12] It seeks to find the meaning established through exegesis, the text's grammatical structure, and sensitivity to its genre. By exegeting Col 1, Steven Smith declared, "The point is clear: Christ is everything because he is unique. Christ is not the highest priority, nor is He the first among others. He stands alone as the center of everything."[13] This subsequent approach aligns with the text serving as the exegetical meaning, the structure as the basic linguistic meaning, and the authorial intent as the emotional design of the text.[14]

### *Convictional Aim*

Furthermore, building on the necessity of preaching that is faithful to exposition, J. Josh Smith, in his book *Preaching for a Verdict*, brought to the conversation the most significant issue within the text: the call to respond. He asserted, "Exhortation is built on the foundation that God has spoken, and His Word is inspired. When we hold the Bible in our hands, we hold a record of what God has said, and we can be confident in its inspiration and inerrancy."[15] He asserted that preaching is set apart from teaching by "calling for a verdict."[16] The exhortation is the call to the will, not just the informing of the mind.[17] It is pleading, persuading, and strongly urging the hearer to respond in obedience to the word of God. Smith argued, "If God has spoken, and he has spoken for a purpose, the responsibility of the preacher is to not only preach His Word (2 Tim 4:2) but also to preach so that people might respond to His Word."[18] Smith also urged, "Exhortation is persuading the listener to respond to the call of the text through proclaiming the point of the text by the voice of the text."[19]

12. Smith, *Dying to Preach*, 65.
13. Smith, *Dying to Preach*, 86.
14. Smith, *Recapturing the Voice of God*, 19–21.
15. Smith, *Preaching for a Verdict*, 21.
16. Smith, *Preaching for a Verdict*, 5.
17. Smith, *Preaching for a Verdict*, 1.
18. Smith, *Preaching for a Verdict*, 31.
19. Smith, *Preaching for a Verdict*, 19.

## Theology of Text-Driven Preaching

Text-driven preaching, as aforementioned, is expository in its foundations. The necessity of seeing the meaning of Scripture within its words is the core principle of expository preaching. David Larsen quoted the Second Helvetic Confession when he asserted, "*Praedicatio verbi dei est verbum dei* ('The preaching of the Word of God is the Word of God'). To the extent that a sermon says what the Word of God says, that sermon is the Word of God."[20] This theology undergirds text-driven preaching—the authority of the word of God. Robby Gallaty and Steven Smith provided the three axioms of text-driven preaching: "The nature of the Word, the nature of the call, and the nature of the church."[21] However, Smith elucidated the role of the preacher concerning the sermon: "Surrendered communication is a relinquishing of our right to say anything we want any way we want. . . . Surrendering to the text is at all times deferring to Scripture, to the point that the sermon is always an expression of the content and spirit of a particular passage."[22]

Furthermore, it is significant to note that Southern Baptists have consistently held to the elevation of preaching within corporate worship. To that end, they are referred to as people of the Bible due to the prominence of the pulpit and the Bible in worship. This concept has provided the needed thrust to keep expositional preaching alive in many Southern Baptist churches.

Additionally, the heartbeat of the Southern Baptists is the necessity of societal impact through missions and evangelism. This conviction toward missions and evangelism played out through the preaching ministry. Chuck Kelley asserted, "The sermon does more than make the gospel known; the demands of the gospel are made known, and a response is expected."[23] Historically speaking, preaching—focusing on the Southern Baptist perspective—included the proclamation of the truth from Scripture and rhetorical persuasion to respond to that truth in a call to respond. Kelley dubbed this

20. Larsen, *Company of Preachers*, 1:19.

21. Gallaty and Smith, *Preaching*, 7.

22. Smith, *Dying to Preach*, 115.

23. Kelley, *Fuel the Fire*, 54.

call "decisional preaching."[24] R. L. Dabney held that rhetoric is an "art of persuasion" intended to move the hearer toward the desired result.[25]

This preaching conviction rests upon the theology that the Bible is inerrant, infallible, inspired, and sufficient, and that Scripture is the final authority on life, moral, and spiritual matters. On this notion, W. A. Criswell asserted, "The Bible is our authority. If God has spoken, then, obviously, His Word is authoritative. Where the word of the king is, there is power. . . . The Scriptures are the teachings of the divinely authenticated messengers of Jesus Christ. All its doctrines arise from God's self-disclosure to humanity."[26] The goal then of text-driven preaching is to connect to the power-laden word of God. The word that illuminates the path of the believer (Ps 119:105), that sanctifies (John 17:17), that pierces "the division of soul and spirit" (Heb 4:12), and that produces faith (Rom 10:17). Allen asserted, "Text-driven preachers refuse to let the congregation walk away without understanding what God is saying to them through the text. . . . It is not outside of the text of Scripture but through the text of Scripture that people encounter God."[27] Smith summarized the theology of text-driven preaching when he elucidated, "We re-present the text. The text re-presents Christ. Christ re-presents the Father."[28] Therefore, the text-driven preacher seeks, as his end, to facilitate an encounter between God and the hearer through the transformative power of God's words, as recorded in Scripture.

## *God Has Spoken*

The means through which God brought all things into existence rests upon his spoken word. Peter Adam asserted, "God speaks, and his words are powerful, effective, and creative of reality. The God who speaks is the God who acts through his words."[29] God's chosen medium of creation weaves through the tapestry of Scripture how he reveals himself. John Stott communicated this theological concept a decade earlier when he stated that God "communicated with his people by speech. . . . It is important to add

24. Kelley, *Fuel the Fire*, 54.
25. Dabney, *Evangelical Eloquence*, 233.
26. Criswell, *Why I Preach*, 192.
27. David L. Allen, introduction to Akin et al., *Text-Driven Preaching*, 8.
28. Smith, *Recapturing the Voice of God*, 14.
29. Adam, *Speaking God's Words*, 15.

that the speech of God was related to his activity: he took the trouble to explain what he was doing."[30] God's action accompanied his speech.

Mark Dever and Greg Gilbert wrote, "From the first page of the Bible, words are enormously important to the God who made the Universe."[31] They explained the theology of God's design to know him and his purposes through his word. The chief example of the Old Testament is found in Gen 1 where God spoke and life sprang forth. Moreover, Gen 2 establishes that God breathed life into his *imago Dei*. Mark Dever and Greg Gilbert stated, "When God creates and gives life, He does so through His Word."[32] The fundamental means by which God interacted with his creation was through words.

Moreover, as recorded in Gen 3, the result of the fall ushered in a new era of communion with God. Where once he spoke directly with mankind, post-fall, he appointed mediators to speak on his behalf. The concept of the *protoevangelium*—or first gospel—sets the redemptive course of the whole of Scripture. Christ's sacrifice accompanies the redemptive nature of Scripture through the cross. Larsen declared, "[The Bible] has an extraordinary unity. . . . God is seen on the earliest pages of Scripture when immediately after the sin of our first parents, God comes seeking them. He brings a promise (the *protoevangelium* of Genesis 3:15)."[33] The redemptive nature of the judgment over Adam and Eve's transgression echoes throughout Scripture.

Through his words, God revealed himself—his divine attributes and characteristics—and his intended purposes for his creation.[34] The implication of God speaking rests firmly on his divine revelation of himself and on his acting through power consistently with his character and nature. God is not holy because he acts holy; he is Holy and, therefore, acts consistent with who he is. The distinction is clear that God speaks through his chosen means of communicating with his creation—the canon of Scripture. Hershael York appealed to the text, stating, "Only when we believe that God has spoken will we dare to speak in His name, and only when we believe that we can understand what He has said will we speak confidently."[35]

30. Stott, *Between Two Worlds*, 65.

31. Dever and Gilbert, *Preach*, 13.

32. Dever and Gilbert, *Preach*, 30.

33. Larsen, *Evangelism Mandate*, 15.

34. Tripp, *War of Words*, 8.

35. See Hershael W. York, "Communication Theory and Text-Driven Preaching," in

### *It Is Written*

Next, Adam stated, "What we have in Scripture is the revealed and preserved words of God."[36] He proceeded to argue for the unity contained within Scripture throughout generations. God's chosen means to communicate the redemptive nature of his purpose was initially through spoken words that transcended time, and later through written words. He wrote, "If God's acts in history are of saving significance not only for generations who are involved in them, but also for future generations, then God's explanation of the meaning of the acts will also be of significance for future generations."[37]

Further illustrating the redemptive connection woven through all of Scripture, Graeme Goldsworthy wrote, "In a remarkable way, the resurrection is portrayed as the event that encapsulates and fulfills all the theological themes of the Old Testament." He continued, "The Bible shows us that God is lawful and that the freedom we have in Christ is not lawless."[38] The Bible reveals the consistency of God's character and nature through the ages.

### *Preach the Word*

Then, Adam connected the concept of preaching to the ministry of the word of God. He contended, "[Preaching] is not mere teaching; it is teaching which achieves the purpose of God in changing people's lives."[39] To preach the word is to communicate the message of God toward the end of transformative change in the congregants' lives. Haddon Robinson stated that sermons "live only when they are preached. A sermon ineptly delivered arrives stillborn."[40] The preaching of the word brings life to the text of Scripture only when utterly dependent upon the Holy Spirit's guidance and Scripture itself. Neglecting that dependence leads to stale sermons devoid of the power to bring about eternal transformation. Smith argued that preaching is "re-presenting the Word of God. We are not to make things up.

---

Akin et al., *Text-Driven Preaching*, 226.

36. Adam, *Speaking God's Words*, 27.

37. Adam, *Speaking God's Words*, 30.

38. Goldsworthy, *Preaching the Whole Bible*, 6.

39. Adam, *Speaking God's Words*, 30.

40. Robinson, *On Biblical Preaching*, 149.

. . . We speak because God has already revealed Himself in His Son, and His Son has revealed Himself in His Word."[41]

Peter Adam asserted that to preach the word is to set Scripture as the sermon's content and illuminate its usefulness to the congregation to reveal "truths about God and how we ought to live in response to God's revelation."[42] Moreover, the apostle Paul charged Timothy to "preach the word" (2 Tim 4:2) and thereby minister the word of Christ to combat false teachings. Ultimately, Charles Simeon illuminated that the ministry of the word, through preaching, humbles the sinner, exalts the Savior, and promotes holiness.[43] Richard Lischer argued, "The point [of preaching] is not to tell bunches of substitute stories or to recount meaningful experiences that are vaguely analogous to God's story but to tell that one story as creatively and powerfully as possible so that present-day communities will live it."[44]

This level of impact and conviction depends wholly upon the move of the Holy Spirit through the proclamation of the message of Christ. Bill Bennett declared, "God accomplishes His purposes in the believer's life by two instruments: the Word of God and the Spirit."[45] The efficacious nature of Scripture's transformative power is a divine mystery wrapped up in the ministry of the Holy Spirit. The key to impactful preaching lies in the preacher's dependence on the Holy Spirit and submission to God's revelation through Scripture.

## The Text-Driven Preaching Model

The text-driven preaching model—the substance, structure, and spirit—seeks to re-present the text of Scripture as it would have been to the original audience. As an outgrowth of expository preaching, text-driven preaching holds that the original author sets the substance of the sermon.[46] Text-driven preaching is a theological approach that emphasizes the primacy of the biblical text in shaping the sermon. It seeks to allow the biblical passage

41. Smith, *Recapturing the Voice of God*, 1.

42. Adam, *Speaking God's Words*, 30.

43. Simeon, *Genesis to Leviticus*, xxi.

44. Lischer, *Theology of Preaching*, 90.

45. See Bill Bennett, "The Secret of Powerful Preaching," in Akin et al., *Text-Driven Preaching*, 60.

46. Robinson, *On Biblical Preaching*, 5.

to drive the message rather than imposing external themes or agendas. By adhering to these principles, text-driven preachers aim to honor the authority and sufficiency of Scripture, ensuring that their sermons are faithful to God's word. This approach contrasts with topical preaching, in which the sermon is built around a specific theme or topic, potentially leading to selective use of Scripture.

### *The Substance of the Text*

Beginning with the substance of the text compels the preacher to understand the author's intended meaning to the original hearers.[47] The preacher must ask, "What is the text talking about?" The answer to this question must be the focus and drive of the sermon. The substance becomes the meaning derived from the text—i.e., the exegesis. In true expository fashion, the importance of text-driven preaching lies in explaining the text.[48] The answer to the question rests firmly in the author's intent, which requires an exegetical study of the text. In understanding the substance of the text, the preacher must lay a foundation in its exegesis. David Allen Black says this about exegesis:

> Exegesis involves looking at the text from three different angles. First, the preacher must stand above the text, getting a bird's-eye view of the whole. Then, they must look inside the text, standing within it and discerning its meaning using all the available exegetical tools. Moreover, the preacher must stand under the text, ready to obey it and to teach it in a way that applies its message to others.[49]

Seeing the text from all facets allows the preacher to capture the central idea. This main idea serves as the aim of the sermon.

Furthermore, Grant Osborne demonstrated that grammar, semantics, and syntax are interdependent and cannot exist in isolation.[50] For example, words possess within themselves a semantic range of definitions. To narrow down the author's intended meaning is to expand the scope from words to sentences. Still, there exists some ambiguity when evaluating sentences.

47. Smith, "Essential Elements."

48. Robinson, *On Biblical Preaching*, 7.

49. See David Allen Black, "Exegesis for the Text-Driven Sermon," in Akin et al., *Text-Driven Preaching*, 137.

50. Osborne, *Hermeneutical Spiral*, 57.

The semantic range of meaning of words calls for the fuller examination of words in their connection with paragraphs. Ultimately, paragraph examination leads to an understanding of the pericope of the text. I. A. Richards declared, "No word can be judged as to whether it is good or bad, correct or incorrect, beautiful or ugly, or anything else that matters to the writer, in isolation."[51]

Within the pericope of the text, the nuanced meaning of each word is found. The interconnection of the words illuminates the original author's intended meaning. Capturing the substance of the text is to exegete the text until the unifying meaning is understood. Smith defined the substance as the meaning of the text.[52] Therefore, understanding the text's meaning requires exegesis. Furthermore, only through proper exegesis can text-driven preaching communicate the meaning of a passage, as intended by God, to the hearer.[53]

The text's main idea can only flourish if the preacher allows the text to guide the sermon. This guiding happens through grasping the deeper meaning of the text, wrestling with the change God is exhorting his people toward, and communicating what God is speaking to the specific context of the local body.[54] Exegesis serves as the battleground for understanding authorial intent. Robinson stated, "When God spoke in the Scriptures, he addressed women and men as they were, where they were. . . . Inappropriate application can be as destructive as inept exegesis."[55]

Therefore, expositional text-driven preaching follows clearly defined movements. These movements serve as hermeneutical road markers that keep the preacher in step with Scripture and the author's intent. Words mean things. Osborne articulated three specific levels of hermeneutics: what the text means, what it means to the reader, and how to communicate that meaning in a modern context.[56] He described the whole enterprise as exegesis, devotional reflection, and the sermon. The preacher must begin with the exegesis of the text—the author's meaning for the original audience, the theological reflection on the cross, and, finally, the application of

51. Richards, *Philosophy of Rhetoric*, 51.

52. Smith, *Recapturing the Voice of God*, 2.

53. See David L. Allen, "Preparing a Text-Driven Sermon," in Akin et al., *Text-Driven Preaching*, 134.

54. Robinson, *On Biblical Preaching*, 10.

55. Robinson, *On Biblical Preaching*, 11.

56. Osborne, *Hermeneutical Spiral*, 22.

the text to the modern audience. Exegesis must begin with a high view of Scripture, holding that the Bible is what God has spoken, and preaching must communicate God's words.[57] Therefore, proper exegesis is to draw out of the text what it means—in stark contrast to eisegesis, which reads the interpreter's predetermined meaning into a text.[58]

Therein lie three inherent dangers for the preacher. First, attempting to go from the text directly to the modern audience results in legalism. This approach results in an author-centered hermeneutic, like that introduced by Friedrich Schleiermacher.[59] This approach misrepresents the text by omitting its historical, literary, and semantic context. The result is biblical foibles and half-truths, resulting in an inconsistent hermeneutic. Ultimately, the significance of what Scripture means is lost. Richards stated, "What a word means is the missing parts of the context from which it draws its delegated efficacy."[60] Neglecting context lends itself to a logical progression that ends in reductionism. David Helm compared this approach to "using the Bible the way a drunk uses a lamp stand—for support and not illumination."[61] Therefore, the preacher simplifies the complexities of the context into a psychological study that connects the original author to the modern audience. The result is reinforcing dogmatic conclusions about strict dos and don'ts.

Second, moving from the text straight to theological reflection on the cross ends in hyperspiritualization. The danger in hyperspiritualization lies in allegorizing. Allegorizing is applying various levels of meaning to a passage that Scripture never intended to be applied to that text.[62] Therein lies the significance of the historical and literary context. Helm questioned "whether preachers can connect Old Testament passages to Christ without undermining what it meant to the original audience."[63] The breadth of understanding must flow from the context (history and language) and the content (what was said).[64] The connection to the gospel rests firmly on the passage's context and its dependence on the revelation that comes

57. York and Decker, *Preaching with Bold Assurance*, 19.

58. Osborne, *Hermeneutical Spiral*, 57.

59. Osborne, *Hermeneutical Spiral*, 468.

60. Richards, *Philosophy of Rhetoric*, 35.

61. Helm, *Expositional Preaching*, 24.

62. Osborne, *Hermeneutical Spiral*, 294.

63. Helm, *Expositional Preaching*, 67.

64. Fee and Stuart, *How to Read the Bible*, 31.

only through the power of the Holy Spirit. Osborne alluded to the tension between external clarity (what the text says) and internal clarity (illumination from the Holy Spirit).[65]

Third, moving from a historical audience straight to a modern one results in moralism. Richards pointed out that divorcing the historical context in favor of the modern context would create a rivalry between the two.[66] Further, Helm showed the danger of applying prescriptively from descriptive passages, leading to imperative legalism.[67] Proper hermeneutics must balance the original audience's understanding of the text with that of the modern audience. Gordon Fee and Douglas Stuart posed, "The most important question of historical context has to do with the occasion and purpose of each biblical book and its various parts."[68] Essentially, proper exegesis cannot bypass the original audience's understanding.

However, the complete work of exegesis must touch upon all four destinations—the author's meaning, the original audience's understanding, the theological reflection from the whole of Scripture, and the implications for the modern audience—within a preacher's sermon preparation and delivery. Osborne noted, "The most important thing is to base the application or contextualization on the text's intended meaning."[69] The order of operations is clear. The preacher must first understand the text's meaning within its proper context. Then, the preacher must strive to communicate that understanding meaningfully. For this reason, text-driven preaching offers the best way to recapture the text's meaning.

### *The Structure of the Text*

The structure of the text suggests that the author's structure of words further reinforces meaning.[70] The structure builds upon the pericope of the text and applies that structure to the preacher's communication. Essentially, the semantic structure of the words used by the original author holds meaning and significance to the text. Smith states that if the "definition of the inspiration and inerrancy of Scripture holds to verbal plenary inspiration,

65. Osborne, *Hermeneutical Spiral*, 27.
66. Richards, *Philosophy of Rhetoric*, 39.
67. Helm, *Expositional Preaching*, 59.
68. Fee and Stuart, *How to Read the Bible*, 31.
69. Osborne, *Hermeneutical Spiral*, 441.
70. See Smith, "Essential Elements."

it means that God not only ordered the content of Scripture, but He also ordered the shape of Scripture."[71] The logical context of Scripture's order plays a foundational role in interpretation. The structural organization of the text illuminates the rhetorical devices employed by the original author to reinforce the main idea.[72]

To this end, linguistics plays a crucial role in biblical interpretation by providing tools and methodologies to understand the languages of the Bible. Through grammar, syntax, and semantics, linguistics guides the interpretation of the original author's intended meaning to convey the text's meaning accurately. Dabney asserted, "No passage of Scripture is suitable for a text which does not contain a distinct and important point. Because a sentence is a part of that Scripture which is declared to be all inspired and all profitable, it does not follow that it is a suitable proposition to furnish instruction for a sermon."[73] His contention rests upon the necessity for linguistic analysis of the text to ensure the proper representation of the pericope of the text. All communication attempts to affect emotions, introduce ideas, or affect behavior.[74]

Examining the text's grammar—or phonology and morphology—allows preachers to analyze the biblical languages' structure and sound systems. Understanding grammar enables the reconstruction of pronunciations and the understanding of word formations. Osborne noted, "Grammar is the key to word meaning, and semantic analysis is dependent upon it."[75] Understanding word pronunciations and formations provides guardrails to prevent from stepping into root fallacies. D. A. Carson identified, "One of the most enduring errors, the root fallacy presupposes that every word actually has a meaning bound up with its shape or its components."[76] The essence of the need to evaluate phonology is the identification of patterns of speech that illuminate contextual meanings. Furthermore, the study of morphology examines the structure of words and how those structures inform meaning.

71. Smith, "Essential Elements."

72. Osborne, *Hermeneutical Spiral*, 51.

73. Dabney, *Evangelical Eloquence*, 99–100.

74. John C. Tuggy, "Semantic Paragraph Patterns," in Black et al., *Linguistics and New Testament Interpretation*, 46.

75. Osborne, *Hermeneutical Spiral*, 63.

76. Carson, *Exegetical Fallacies*, 28.

Moreover, syntax focuses on the arrangement of words and phrases and the rules that govern them. Word usage is vital for interpreting sentence structures and understanding the flow of thought in biblical passages. The grammatical rules of the original languages clarify the text's meaning. Carson illustrated the importance of syntactical study: "In complex syntactical units, there is a greater number of variables than in single words, and therefore a greater number of things to go wrong."[77] Therefore, a syntactical study of Scripture should examine sentence structure. This study includes construction, word arrangement, and the hierarchical organization of phrases and clauses. It involves understanding the relationships between subjects, verbs, objects, and other sentence elements.

In addition to the syntactical relationships between words, semantics delves into the meanings of words and phrases, which is essential given the vast temporal and cultural differences between biblical texts and contemporary readers. Linguistics enables interpreters to grasp the nuances and connotations of ancient words and expressions by studying the historical and cultural contexts of language use. Semantics explores the meaning of words and how they relate to one another.[78] It includes understanding how the meanings of individual words combine to form the meanings of larger linguistic units, such as phrases and sentences. It studies how syntactic structures influence meaning and how context affects interpretation. Semantics also explores various meaning relations, such as entailment (where one statement logically follows from another), contradiction (where one statement negates another), and ambiguity (where a word or phrase has multiple interpretations).[79]

Moreover, it is worth noting that pragmatics examines language in use and the context of communication. Context helps us understand the intentions behind biblical narratives and the rhetorical strategies employed by the authors. Linguistics offers a systematic approach to uncovering the layers of meaning within the Bible and communicating that information in an accessible and relevant way for modern audiences. Communication then stands at the forefront of preaching, and the text's structure matters. Matthew McKellar asserted, "Many communication theorists assert that

77. Carson, *Exegetical Fallacies*, 65.

78. See John C. Tuggy, "Semantic Paragraph Patterns," in Black et al., *Linguistics and New Testament Interpretation*, 51.

79. See John C. Tuggy, "Semantic Paragraph Patterns," in Black et al., *Linguistics and New Testament Interpretation*, 50–51.

meanings do not exist in words by themselves but in the minds of persons who interpret them."[80]

### *The Spirit of the Text*

The spirit of the text is the author's intended "feel," shaped by the genre.[81] This notion holds that preaching should reflect the text's genre—both in structure and in feel. Gallaty and Smith caution, "However, genre alone does not dictate the mood of the text."[82] Genre helps guide the analysis of the text by applying a literary genre. Robert Vogel contended, "[A literary genre's] distinguishing rules and characteristics help the interpreter/expositor know how to approach the text of that genre and, consequently, how to interpret and explain what is written."[83]

At the heart of the text's spirit is understanding the methods of interpreting the fundamental types of the genre—narrative, procedural, expository, and hortatory.[84] For example, to preach a lighthearted message from Lamentations or Jeremiah does a disservice to the passage's meaning. Both instances reflect the deserved judgment, yet each offers a glimmer of hope in the new covenant. The preacher would do well to feel the weight of the words of judgment to come and the hope woven in. The essence of understanding the spirit of the text is to see the revelation of God as originally intended for the original audience.[85] To get the substance and structure but miss the feel of the text is to miss an aspect of the meaning.[86]

## Conclusion

Ultimately, the notion of expository preaching holds its footing in the annals of history. From Origen and John Chrysostom, William Perkins and Richard Baxter, W. A. Criswell and Adrian P. Rogers, David L. Allen and

80. McKellar, "Elements of Persuasion," 13.

81. See Smith, "Essential Elements."

82. Gallaty and Smith, *Preaching*, 32.

83. Robert Vogel, "Biblical Genres and the Text-Driven Sermon," in Akin et al., *Text-Driven Preaching*, 167.

84. See David L. Allen, "The Rules of the Game," in Robinson and Larson, *Art and Craft*, 237.

85. Robinson, *On Biblical Preaching*, 47.

86. See Smith, "Essential Elements."

Steven W. Smith—commitment to expository preaching is rooted in taking a text, explaining it, and applying it.[87] Faithfulness to the text of Scripture is the aim of every text-driven expositor. The preacher must speak when Scripture speaks and remain silent when the text is silent. This book shows that Paul's commendation of Timothy to preach the word anchors in the necessity of reproof, rebuke, and exhortation—the summons. Each of those verbs demands a decision that rests at the feet of the hearer in response to the gospel. Although not explicitly stated, preaching for a response is implicit in Paul's chosen verbs. To reprove serves to convince; to rebuke reveals the hearers' need in their dire state; and to exhort is to urge the hearer back to the gospel. Each of these verbs calls the hearer to change their mind and—in the case of exhortation—to turn back.

87. Walker, *Let the Text Talk*, 134.

# CHAPTER 2

# The Summons of the Text

THE HEART OF TEXT-DRIVEN exposition lies in the pursuit of textual faithfulness in preaching. We must wrestle with the meaning of the text in the study chamber with an ever-watchful eye toward faithfulness to the authorial intent. Building on the previous chapter, this chapter seeks to show that the study of God's word culminates in the whole exegetical process, which naturally reveals the summons of the text. The substance is where the Holy Spirit reveals the main idea of the text. The substance, structure, spirit, and summons come into focus as the culmination of the whole work of exegesis. Grant Osborne stated, "Unless we can grasp the whole before attempting to dissect the parts, interpretation is doomed from the start."[1] We must strive to understand the nuances of context to reinforce our understanding of the original meaning for the intended audience, thereby revealing a universal truth applicable to the church today. When the original author employs a concept, it is vitally important that we strive to bridge the gap in time between the original author's culture and the audience to whom we are addressing today. Understanding the main idea requires first gathering what it meant to the original author and audience.

Imagine, for a moment, that our exegesis is like archery. Each arrow then represents the process of working out the exegesis of a passage. In order for an arrow to fly straight, it must have specific characteristics. First, arrows must be straight. Straightness is an essential characteristic for consistent flight. Without consistency, the archer cannot repeat their process to improve their accuracy. Second, the arrows used must be consistent in weight. The weight difference between arrows changes the archer's ability

1. Osborne, *Hermeneutical Spiral*, 37.

and, therefore, their accuracy. Third, the arrows must have the correct spine or stiffness. The stiffness of the arrow becomes an important factor in controlling the flex of the shaft during flight. Each of these factors contributes to the archer's overall consistency. Consistency in exegesis is as vitally important as the consistency of the arrow to an archer. However, the composition of an arrow alone is insufficient to accomplish the task of hitting the mark. The more consistent we are with our use of language, reference to historical context, and so on, the more our exegetical precision—the straightness of the shaft, the consistency of weight, and the composition of the spine of the arrow—determines accuracy.

Building on the substance, we find that the text's structure further reveals its meaning. It essentially further drives and reinforces its meaning. Language analysis must inform the meaning of the text. Words mean things, and it is their structure that gives clarity. The grammatical context of words narrows their semantic range of meaning. Our understanding of the context deepens as we examine sentences, paragraphs, and the author's complete thoughts, presented in a structured format. The structure of the words must reinforce the substance of the text's meaning, or something has gone terribly awry.

Imagine that the bow riser is the structural analysis of the text. The bow riser holds the arrow in place for firing. There are distinct characteristics of the riser that are important to the archer. First, the bow riser must reduce vibration and torsion. Effective vibration dampening reduces the wobble in the arrow when it takes flight. Additionally, torsion control prevents the arrow from twisting. Second, the geometry of the bow determines how the bow reacts to the torque of the drawstring and its subsequent release. Finally, the riser should be light enough not to cause additional arm strain when fully drawn. Similarly, the structure informs the semantic range of meaning of the complete thought in the passage. It is because words hold specific meanings in their context. Words, in their proper structure and context, can never mean what they would never have meant to the original author. Therefore, the more stable the arrow is in the riser, the more accurate the shot, just as the stability of the word structure gives us the necessary platform upon which the Holy Spirit speaks through the text.

Nevertheless, the arrow, seated correctly in the riser, can make no change apart from the power of the tension of the string. Therein is the power of genre sensitivity. The drawstring of the bow must provide strength, power, and low stretch while offering a smooth release. First, the strength of the material withstands the force placed upon it. Second, the power of the drawstring launches the arrow through energy transference. Third, the low stretch prevents creep, or elongation of the string, within the drawstring. Finally, the smooth release provides consistency in the archer's form. Recapturing the feel of the text imbues the exegesis with the biblical authority, emotive power, and theological depth to affect the mind, emotions, and will of the listener. The spirit of the text further clarifies its meaning through literary genre analysis. Peter Adam declared, "Our preaching should convey, not reduce, the intellectual and emotional impact of our text."[2] Essentially, the spirit, or feel, of the text helps to maintain a greater understanding of the substance and structure.

The make of the arrow, the placement on the riser, and the tension of the string all contribute to a successful shot. However, apart from using sights, your aim is suspect. The summons then stands as the aim of the text (the sights). In other words, to what is the passage calling the hearer to respond? The summons seeks to affect the mind, emotions, and will through the reproof, rebuke, and exhortation toward godly obedience worked out in the hearer's life. The summons of the text further illuminates its meaning by capturing the revelation of truth about God. Knowing the aim of the text's call infuses the sermon with precision of purpose. The summons of the text must work in concert with the substance, structure, and spirit of the text. In that way, the summons further reinforces the meaning of the text discovered thus far. It is interesting to note that each of these depends on the other. These are not necessarily sequential operations; instead, you work through one, move on to the next, and then revisit and clarify what you know through what you are learning.

Therefore, each of these aspects (substance, structure, spirit, and summons) establishes our consistency in the interpretation and development of the sermon. Similarly, the precision of shooting compares to how consistently we treat the text. Our consistency depends upon our exegetical methods, structural analysis, sensitivity to the genre, and anchoring to the text's call. However, precision is only part of the issue. Let us say you are at the archery range, and from fifty yards, your precision is an arrow grouping of less than an inch, and your accuracy is hitting the bullseye. You begin to feel pretty good about your abilities. Nevertheless, what if you looked up and all your arrows are in the target two lanes down? Yeah, you hit a target's bullseye, just the wrong one.

2. Adam, *Speaking God's Words*, 97.

The closer to the bullseye, the more accurate our interpretations will be. Precision toward the bullseye is where a deep, convictional dependence upon the Holy Spirit cannot be overstated. The word of God must first permeate our hearts before we can accurately impact the hearts and minds of the congregation. Once an archer releases the arrow, they relinquish control over the arrow. Unlike archery, preaching offers an additional avenue of success—the Holy Spirit. However, consistency in our exegesis (precision) is foundational to our dependence (accuracy) upon the Holy Spirit. Faithfulness to the text is what we aim for, ultimately flowing from our surrender to the Holy Spirit.

Preaching the text faithfully is not merely about explaining what it says but about embodying its call, inviting the congregation to respond and obey. The inclusion of the summons of the text serves as both a faithful extension and a necessary refinement of the text-driven preaching model. Historically, the pulpit has not only proclaimed truth but also compelled response through rhetorical persuasion, echoing prophetic and apostolic traditions inseparable from exhortation. Biblically, Scripture consistently presents God's word as living and active—the call of the summons of the text is displayed in a call to salvation and a call to sanctification. The expectation of obedience in response to the gospel is explicit—the call resonates with the whole person, encompassing the mind, emotions, and will. Theologically, the summons aligns with a robust pneumatology and missional ecclesiology, recognizing that preaching is a Spirit-empowered act that calls upon preachers to preach the word for reproof, rebuke, and exhortation toward repentance, faith, and godly obedience—not merely informing but also transforming. The conclusion drawn from the text is the natural outcome of a faithful, text-driven exposition, given the historical, biblical, and theological evidence presented.

## The Need for the Summons

When we consider Paul's exhortation to Timothy to "preach the word" (2 Tim 4), an issue arises in Steven Smith's text-driven preaching model: the absence of emphasis on the exhortation of the text. To Smith's credit, he identified the need for exhortation when he wrote, "I had taught students explanation, argumentation, and application, but not exhortation. The net result was accuracy without urgency."[3] He rightly identified the potential

3. Gallaty and Smith, *Preaching*, 119.

danger of a lack of urgency in any text-driven approach to preaching that neglects the exhortation. The need for urgency is invariably lost when we neglect exhortation. This charge is not to say that expositional preachers have not successfully captured the essence of the text in their application. Instead, it is to draw attention to the necessity of intentionality. Have you ever preached a sermon and, at the conclusion of the service, knew that something was amiss in the application? We have all been there. What the summons of the text offers is an intentionality in establishing the scriptural foundation that thrusts into the application. Dependence upon Scripture culminates in the necessity of the sermon's conclusion with a call to respond. Ultimately, Steven Smith's discussion of expository preaching concurs with the need for the invitation to follow Christ.[4] This call to follow, as we shall see in later chapters, should not be relegated to salvation only. Instead, it should encompass the exaltation of Christ as both Savior and Lord. Essentially, it is a call to the whole self to be in union with Christ (salvation) as well as in deeper communion with Christ (sanctification). This call to salvation and sanctification is where the text-driven model needs to incorporate the summons' intentionality.

Robby Gallaty argued in *Preaching for the Rest of Us*—Steven Smith's coauthor—that an effective way to engage with the hearer about the invitation is to ask enticing questions.[5] This approach appears to depart from Smith's text-driven philosophy and raises the question, If the invitation should flow from the main idea, what implication is there that it should connect directly to the exhortation? Gallaty wrote that the invitation should connect to the text's central idea. However, if we neglect the connection with the exhortation present within the text, we find ourselves in dangerous waters. This lack of connection becomes problematic, as it neglects Paul's command to reprove, rebuke, and exhort (see 2 Tim 4:2). Attempting to connect the invitation to the main idea without exploring the summons of the text proves an arduous and perilous journey rife with exegetical pitfalls.

Ultimately, the text-driven preaching model provides an exceptional foundation for preaching the text as a re-presenting of the author's intent. The theological foundation of the text-driven preaching model is that God has spoken; the substance elucidates the critical role of exegesis; the structure expounds the linguistic meaning; the spirit explicates the meaning associated with the feel of the text through genre sensitivity; and the

4. Gallaty and Smith, *Preaching*, 119.

5. Gallaty and Smith, *Preaching*, 119.

summons exhorts the hearer to respond to the truth of the person and work of Christ revealed in the text.

## Clarity of the Summons

Furthering the conversation, there appears to be some confusion about how the application draws from text-driven expository sermons. This lack of emphasis on the summons has often led to a conflation of the ideas of application and exhortation. J. Josh Smith rightly brought to the conversation the need to preach the exhortation in his book *Preaching for a Verdict*. He wrote, "The role of exhortation appears to have been overlooked in the past twenty-five years; however, this has not always been the case in the history of the pedagogy of homiletics."[6] Although Smith drew lines for the conversation, some misunderstandings and misgivings still appear to exist regarding the distinction between exhortation and application. We often find ourselves seemingly swapping them. We emphasize the application while neglecting the exhortation of the text. The difficulty in defining the distinction between the two is subtle and discreet. So nuanced are the differences that one could argue that such a distinction is simply semantics. However, I argue that there is great value in clarifying the distinction. There exists a distinction between the two that offers renewed life in our preaching. This new life lies in what he called the four purposes for God speaking to us: self-revelation, relationship, sanctification, and response.[7] I would add that God's call to response deepens the first three purposes, offering greater revelation of himself in relationship through sanctification.

What is more, Steven Smith posited the cause of the confusion in the conversation. He identified that the shift from exhortation to modern application rests in "telling people practically what they can do, with less emphasis on the mandate to respond to God. . . . Without exhortation, application can descend into a stylized self-help sermon."[8] This practical application approach can lead to a self-help approach to the sermon, which can drift from the text's mandate to emphasize salvation and sanctification toward a felt-needs approach in the application. If we jump prematurely to the application for the audience, we can lose sight of God's intended purpose in speaking. We must first understand what the text demands of

6. Smith, *Preaching for a Verdict*, 11.
7. Smith, *Preaching for a Verdict*, 25–28.
8. Gallaty and Smith, *Preaching*, 121.

us in light of God's revelation of himself through the relationship restored by Christ, for our holiness and sanctification in him. Without a scriptural foundation, application is prone to drift from theological orthodoxy and Christ-centeredness.

To correct this course, we must look at Scripture as the anchor of our faith. We must embrace the truth that right practice comes from correct doctrine. The right doctrine comes from correct theology. Moreover, correct theology comes from the proper interpretation of Scripture. Specifically, we should look at where Paul commands Timothy to reprove, rebuke, and exhort in connection with preaching the word. Paul established the weight of his charge by invoking God himself as the underlying authority. Explicit is the charge to proclaim the message of Christ, and the result rests in the appeal to the mind, emotions, and will of the hearer of the word. Implicit is the idea that exhortation is simply the truth in the text to which a person must respond. The exhortation re-presents the call to physical action, the call to adjust a view of God, or both.

Fundamentally, Scripture is the revelation of God to mankind. The implications of each passage in context call for deeper worship of God through the revelation of himself. Steven Smith rightly stated, "Once the truth is clear, the preacher has the freedom and responsibility to press the truth home to the hearer in a way that is compelling, even forceful."[9] Moreover, this idea of the summons rests upon the notion that it is the truth in the text to which a person must respond. The summons re-presents the call to transformation by adjusting our view of God, fostering a more profound affection for God, and encouraging us to transform our physical responses. Fundamentally, Scripture is the revelation of God to mankind. The implications of each passage in context call for deeper worship of God through his revelation. This understanding implies a perspicuity of meaning from each text—a faithful worship of God through deeper faith in him by the greater revelation of himself. That meaning connects to a profound dependence upon and a prioritized relationship with Jesus.

At the heart of the summons lies reproof, rebuke, and exhortation. At the heart of this notion of the summons lies a call for clarity in understanding the nuanced distinction between the summons and the application. The summons is what the text commands of the hearer—what to do. The application contrasts how the hearer applies the summons to their lives—how to do it. David Helm refers to this process as synthesizing what is said and

9. Smith, *Dying to Preach*, 171.

applying it. He asserted, "Synthesis must be done. And the biblical expositors who do it well do so, in part, because of the contextualized attention they give to the audience, arrangement, and application."[10]

### *The Summons Is What the Text Commands*

Specifically, the summons of the text is the truth statement revealed in Scripture, exhorting the hearer to respond.[11] This concept is what I am calling the "whatness" of the text. Fundamentally, Scripture reveals the character and nature of God for the worship and submission to God. Essentially, each text, within its proper context, seeks as its aim to call its hearers to the worship of God, for he is worthy. We must ask ourselves, What is this text showing us about God? The Scriptures are our authoritative source for knowing God.

The summons, then, stands upon that biblical authority. This dependence upon Scripture reveals the timeless truth about God that the text demands of the hearer. Proper exegesis serves as our means of getting to what the text calls. As elucidated in Scripture, the truth statement about the person and work of Christ should convict the hearer to respond. This revelation is connected to the text's central idea. It serves as what the Holy Spirit commands of the hearer—a change in mind, heart, and will. Theologically, the truth of Christ prompts the hearer to respond either (1) in faith or rejection of Christ's salvation and lordship or (2) in more profound commitment to Christ through sanctification.[12]

At its core, the summons confronts our worldview with the truth of Scripture. If Scripture asserts the truth contrary to what we have held, we must change. The summons confronts the lies we hold with the truth from Scripture. This revelation ultimately leads to a Spirit-led obedience. As Jesus said, "Sanctify them in the truth; Your word is truth" (John 17:17). Scripture sanctifies through the revelation of truth. J. Josh Smith notes, "The goal of the sermon is to communicate what the text is saying in the same way the text is saying it. In other words, everything in a given sermon is a reflection of what is given in the text."[13]

10. Helm, *Expositional Preaching*, 89.
11. Adam, *Speaking God's Words*, 24–25.
12. Smith, *Preaching for a Verdict*, 26–28.
13. Smith, *Preaching for a Verdict*, 94.

Finally, the "whatness" of the summons should stand upon the passionate persuasion of the preacher. Text-driven exposition must be grounded in the preacher's *ethos*, *logos*, and *pathos*. This spiritual rhetoric is part of the whole. The effect is to stay faithful to the text to allow the Holy Spirit to call and draw upon the hearer's mind, emotions, and will (through reproof, rebuke, and exhortation). The key focus of the summons is to fully capture the text-driven sermon so that the natural conclusion rests upon the Holy Spirit–inspired call from the text.

### *The Application Is How to Respond*

Furthermore, the application involves moving from the summons—the what to do—to the practical application of the hearer—the how to do it. J. Josh Smith wrote, "Preachers are called not just to communicate information, but to help people see how that information applies to their lives. Preachers are bridging the gap between God's truth and the world as it is. Application answers the question, How does this truth affect my life?"[14] This concept is what I call the "howness" of the text. How do we take the truths outlined in Scripture and apply them to our daily lives? Application is not about behavior modification; rather, it is about transformation by the Holy Spirit actively lived out in our lives. For example, Jesus said, "Love your enemies, do good to those who hate you, bless those who curse you, pray for those who mistreat you" (Luke 6:27b–28). This command does not stand alone as a call to transformed behavior. However, it is a call to look to the revelation of God's kindness toward "evil men" (Luke 6:35b). Therefore, in light of God's demonstrated character, we live looking to God's reward as sons of the Most High.

Additionally, given that the primary goal of the text-driven sermon is to reveal the text's central meaning, we can confidently state that the implicit connection reveals Christ. Moreover, the central idea reveals Christ, who calls the hearer to change through salvation or greater sanctification. Capturing the summons of the text naturally leads to a greater application for the hearer by anchoring on the universal spiritual truth. The application is where the preacher connects the theological and biblical truths presented in the message to the everyday lives of the congregation, offering concrete steps and insights for applying these truths. Essentially, returning to our aforementioned Luke 6 example, the application can be to look to Christ in

14. Smith, *Preaching for a Verdict*, 105.

the daily relational struggles. We all have those people we struggle to like. God's call is that, in the same way he demonstrated mercy toward us, we should strive to demonstrate the mercy we received toward those around us.

It is important to draw a point of caution as we proceed. When the application is divorced from the main idea, the audience's felt needs take priority over Scripture. Every summons leads to an application as its outcome, but not all applications directly tie back to the original summons. While the application seeks to inspire and urge action within the hearers' lives, only the text's summons offers the universal, Holy Spirit–inspired power through which lasting change occurs.

Felt-needs preaching can subvert Scripture by placing it in submission to the hearer rather than the hearer being submitted to Scripture. It can subtly shift the focus of meaning from the revelation of God to a moral-therapeutic-deistic or even an optimistic-narcissistic-deistic message, effectively jettisoning the redemptive necessity of the text. This ambiguity leaves the congregation internally focused, spiritually malnourished, and theologically shallow in their faith. Furthermore, the preacher commits the grievous sin of exegetical adultery—unfaithfulness to the text. In time, the preacher's felt-needs sermon erodes biblical literacy, distorts the character of God, and results in a consumeristic congregation. Ultimately, the danger does not just lie in what is said but in what is omitted. Dietrich Bonhoeffer wrote, "Cheap grace is the preaching of forgiveness without requiring repentance, baptism without church discipline, communion without confession. Cheap grace is grace without discipleship, grace without the cross, grace without Jesus Christ, living and incarnate."[15] What is left unsaid is sin, repentance, the glory of Christ through the gospel, and our most profound need for reconciliation with a holy God.

### *Differentiating the Summons, Application, Invitation, and Altar Call*

The summons stands as the core command of the text of what God demands. This call stands as the "whatness" of the text. The summons is the divine call of the text to embrace the truth of God proclaimed. It answers the question, What is God asking of the audience? The application stands as the practical and contextualized means of living out the truth of Scripture.

15. Bonhoeffer, *Cost of Discipleship*, 44.

This contextualization stands as the "howness" of the text. The application is the individualistic plan for living out the universal truth proclaimed.

The distinction between the summons and the application is crucial. The difference in the "whatness" of the summons and the "howness" of the application preserves the biblical authority of the text. In addition, it compels the hearer to respond in their specific context faithfully to the message of Scripture. When preachers blur the two, sermons risk becoming vague exhortations with no practical traction or overly pragmatic talks that lose their biblical weight. Clearly articulating what God is calling us to—repentance, faith, obedience—and then showing how that call can be lived out, the preacher faithfully proclaims God's voice and the human context in which it is heard.

The historic understanding of invitation has blurred with that of an altar call. Therefore, adding clarity ensures that, moving forward, we are all on the same page. The invitation stands as an appeal to the hearers, inviting them to respond to the sermon. This invitation typically involves engaging with the heart, mind, and will, urging the listener to respond through internal reflection and prayer. While this could include an altar call, it does not necessitate one. The invitation is predominantly viewed from an evangelistic bent, inviting hearers to place their trust in Christ. However, this can also be an invitation to reflect upon the sermon in the moment. It has, within the Baptist tradition, customarily been an opportunity to seek prayer from the pastors, deacons, or elders of the church.

In contrast, the altar call is a specific method used in the invitation. It literally calls for a physical response to come down to the altar and pray. Historically, this has been tied to the idea of public profession, affirming the work of the Holy Spirit in your heart and not denying Christ. In many Christian traditions, this has been viewed as a part of sanctification. The emphasis is grounded in salvation, rededication, and greater commitment to Christ.

For the summons, it is rooted in the notion of an invitation but does not necessitate an altar call. It stands upon Scripture and the call to respond to God. Adrian Rogers wrote, "On the day of Pentecost, Peter preached a great sermon, and then he gave an invitation. . . . The sermon was over. But 'with many other words,' now he's testifying, 'This is what Jesus has done for me.' He's exhorting, 'Let it be done to you' with many other words."[16] The invitation that Peter gave was rooted in his proclamation of Christ from

16. Rogers, *Preaching for Impact*, 75.

the Old Testament. Peter showed Christ from the prophet Joel and from the Davidic psalms. Then, his invitation anchors in placing saving faith in Christ. The Holy Spirit had already pierced their hearts, and he then called them to repentance and baptism. In other words, they were affected by the proclamation of Christ, and the whole approach of the text shows their emotions, minds, and will. But more on that in chapter 6.

For now, let us establish the understanding that Scripture calls for a response, and from that, there are distinct expectations. There is an expectation upon the preacher to handle the word of God rightly. Nevertheless, there is also an expectation on the hearer to respond. It is vitally important that, as a preacher of the gospel, we understand that the only change we can effect is through being a conduit for the Holy Spirit. The best way to be that conduit is through textual faithfulness. Proclaim the word faithfully, intentionally, and expectantly.

## The Expectation upon the Preacher

Textual faithfulness demands that the preacher preach Scripture in its context with an eye toward the Word revealed—Jesus Christ. The summons plays a vital role in preaching, as it bridges the gap between teaching the declaration of biblical truths and expectation in those truths that compels the hearer to respond, ultimately motivating the congregation to live out their faith actively. The primary goal of preaching is to convey God's word, and the summons captures the audience's expectation toward reproof, rebuke, and exhortation for godliness.

The preacher communicates the text's passion and urgency through the summons, allowing the main idea to appeal to the audience's mind, heart, and will. He employs persuasion as a tool for the Holy Spirit to stir conviction and foster a sense of accountability, prompting the audience to reflect on their spiritual state before the revelation of a Holy God. This element of preaching is not merely about delivering information; it is about fostering transformation and encouraging a response to God's message. He must fully recognize the various members of the audience within the congregation—the believer and the unbeliever—and seek to draw out the text's call to each to respond. William Perkins stated that there are "churches with both believers and unbelievers. This is the typical situation in our congregations. Any doctrine may be expounded to them, either from the law or from the gospel, so long as its biblical limitations and circumscriptions are observed."[17]

Moreover, a preacher who is devoid of heartfelt passion in reading the text exacerbates the neglect of the summons. C. Kyle Walker posited,

> If, by the way he reads [the Bible], the preacher can cause the people to understand the Word of God, how important that he learn to read it well! If the preacher can interpret and practically apply the Word of God by the way he reads it, what answer will he make at the judgment bar if, by sheer indifference and wanton neglect of his talent, he fails to become an effective reader?[18]

The preacher's responsibility in delivering an exhortation is profound, as it involves spiritual leadership and genuine care for the congregation. At its core, he must faithfully communicate God's word, ensuring the message aligns with biblical truth while addressing the text's specific call for the audience. This call requires careful study, prayerful preparation, and sensitivity to the Holy Spirit. Additionally, it requires him to provide a challenge to act upon the truth of Scripture—the heart of the summons rests upon the evangelistic and sanctifying invitation.[19]

## The Expectation upon the Hearer

Given the variety in audiences, the intention of the summons is twofold—salvation and sanctification. The first expectation of the summons is to aim for salvation for the unbeliever. Paul attested, "So faith comes from hearing, and hearing by the word of Christ" (Rom 10:17). Apart from the divine power of the Holy Spirit upon the hearts of the unrepentant, no number of words will sway them toward Christ. However, the primary call upon the preacher is to preach the gospel. Puritan William Perkins understood the implication of the spiritual state of his various listeners when he asserted,

> Those who are unbelievers are both ignorant and unteachable. These must first of all be prepared to receive the doctrine of the word. . . . This preparation should be partly by discussing or reasoning with them, in order to become aware of their attitude and disposition, and partly by reproving any obvious sin, so their

17. Perkins, *Art of Prophesying*, 70.
18. Walker, *Let the Text Talk*, 125.
19. Perry and Strubhar, *Evangelistic Preaching*, 106.

> consciences may be aroused and touched with fear that they may become teachable.[20]

Perkins knew that the preacher must be aware of the call to repentance, whether from the weight of judgment under the law of God or from the grace of divine mercy in the gospel. Preachers must reason with unbelievers to help them come to grips with their spiritual needs.

The second expectation of the summons is the necessity of sanctification for the believer. Sanctification through the word of God is essential to the believer's spiritual growth and transformation. Sanctification is being set apart for God, becoming holy, and aligning one's life with his will. The word of God is central to this process, serving as the foundation for moral guidance, spiritual renewal, and a deeper relationship with God.

Scripture reveals God's character, standards, and purposes, providing believers with a clear understanding of what it means to live a holy life. Passages such as John 17:17 highlight that God's word sanctifies believers, which acts as a cleansing agent for the soul, purifying thoughts, attitudes, and actions. The word of God is living and active (Heb 4:12), penetrating hearts and convicting believers of sin. It not only exposes areas of life that need change but also offers encouragement and hope for transformation. By meditating on and obeying Scripture, believers are renewed in their minds (Rom 12:2) and equipped to resist temptation, walk in righteousness, and bear fruit that glorifies God. Walker attested, "Text-driven preaching grows the people's hunger for the Word. . . . Felt needs are often genuine needs. Yet, they are not always the deepest needs. Text-driven preaching trusts that God knows man's deepest needs and, therefore, allows Scripture, rather than man's needs, to set the homiletical agenda."[21]

The summons provides comfort and reassurance, reminding the believer of God's grace, love, and promises. It strengthens the community of believers by nurturing unity in the faith—urging continual repentance and acts of service and providing hope in Christ during challenging times. The summons calls for greater sanctification, calling believers to live Christ-centered lives. On this point, John Piper attested, "[Preachers] must pray and preach so that a new mental framework is created for seeing the world. Ultimately, this is not [the preacher's] doing. God must do it. . . . God

20. Perkins, *Art of Prophesying*, 63.

21. Walker, *Let the Text Talk*, 109.

brings about this new seeing and understanding and believing. But he uses [preachers] to do it."[22]

## Conclusion

The summons within the text is the truth that the author is commending to his hearers. Scripture is the divine revelation of who God is and what he has done. From this understanding, the exhortation of the text commands readers to respond—either by walking in obedience or transforming their view of God. Reflecting on the call for response, D. Martyn Lloyd-Jones argued that the call for decision must be "in the Truth itself, and in the message."[23] That is to say, the passage's main idea should dictate the call to respond. Given that the whole of Scripture reveals Christ, the call to respond should also flow from the structure of the text. Ultimately, the spirit of the text should guide how the sermon addresses the hearer. Therefore, the summons of the text naturally draws from the redemptive nature of the cross. The gospel must be present in the expositor's mind as they exegete the text. Bryan Chapell argued, "Accurate expositors use a magnifying glass and a fish-eye lens, knowing that a magnifying glass can unravel mysteries in a raindrop but fail to expose a storm gathering on the horizon."[24]

Finally, there exists a dichotomy in preaching: the biblical responsibility of the preacher's faithful proclamation and the hearer's expectation to respond to that message. Preachers are entrusted as stewards of God's word, tasked with accurately and faithfully proclaiming its truth without distortion or compromise. However, this responsibility does not exist in isolation. The dynamic nature of preaching assumes that God's word is not merely informational but transformational—it is designed to pierce hearts, convict souls, and inspire action. Jason Meyer stated, "Along with re-presenting God's Word and representing God himself, preaching is concerned that people respond to God and His Word."[25] This interplay—faithful proclamation and responsive hearing—reflects the transformative nature of God's word. The preacher functions as the sower delivering the seed of truth, but the listener becomes the soil. The preacher must plant and cultivate that

22. Piper, *Supremacy of God*, 128.

23. Lloyd-Jones, *Preaching and Preachers*, 296.

24. See Bryan Chapell, "Redemptive-Historic View," in Gibson and Kim, *Homiletics and Hermeneutics*, 5.

25. Meyer, *Preaching*, 250.

seed of truth. Together, this dynamic fulfills the purpose of preaching: glorifying God by leading his people to grow in faith and live out the gospel.

# CHAPTER 3

# Seeing Christ Throughout Scripture

AT THE HEART OF Scripture is the revelation of the character of God, his divine attributes, and his workings toward his creation. In that vein of thought, to see the character, attributes, and workings of God the Father is also to see God the Son and God the Spirit—hence the Trinitarian foundation that is at the heart of orthodox Christianity. Upon this foundation, we can see the divine power and preexistence of God in Gen 1:1 entirely apply to the Godhead. The ubiquity of Christ in Scripture underscores the centrality of Jesus throughout the Bible. This biblical precedent of the person and work of Christ woven throughout Scripture extends from Genesis to Revelation.

From God's revelation of himself, a summons exists—the exaltation of Christ (from the revelation of the Godhead) toward the aim of glorification of the Father with the expressed purpose of salvation and sanctification of a people for his own possession. Further, the early apostolic kerygma exemplifies the necessity of the preacher to proclaim Christ and to call for a response anchored in the summons of the text. Christ is king, and he establishes his kingdom in the hearts of his people through their entrance into his kingdom (salvation) and their submission to his kingship (sanctification).

This chapter will provide a cursory examination of biblical accounts that demonstrate the New Testament use of the Old Testament to reveal and exalt the person and work of Christ. First, this shows that Christ is woven into the fabric of Scripture, revealing his person and work as central to God's redemptive plan. Second, Christ is prefigured and anticipated through various types and prophecies in the Old Testament. Third,

Scripture reveals his character, attributes, and works through the Trinitarian understanding of God. Finally, the redemption thread, as seen in the promise of a redeemer in Gen 3:15, the messianic prophecies, the typology of figures like Melchizedek, David, and the suffering servant, the sacrificial system, the Passover lamb that foreshadowed his ultimate sacrifice, and many more, all point to Christ. John Stott asserted, "This is the main key to the understanding of Scripture. The Bible is God's picture of Jesus. It bears witness to him. So, whenever we are reading the Bible, we must look for Christ."[1]

Coupled to the Old Testament anticipation is the New Testament revelation. The New Testament testifies to Christ's life, death, and resurrection as the culmination of God's plan. The Gospels recount his earthly ministry through his teachings and miracles, emphasizing his role as the Messiah, informed by Scripture and affirmed by his miraculous works. The New Testament Epistles expound on the theological significance of Christ's atoning work. Specifically, the book of Hebrews elucidates his role as the perfect high priest and mediator, anchoring it in the Old Testament.

Finally, New Testament passages proclaiming redemption portray the exalted Christ—the Alpha and Omega—reigning supreme over all creation in various fashions. Throughout Scripture, Christ's presence is ubiquitous, demonstrating that he is the cornerstone of God's revelation and the key to understanding the biblical messages. This chapter looks at three biblical examples of the truth of Jesus revealed throughout Scripture—the declaration of Jesus and the road to Emmaus, Phillip and the Ethiopian eunuch, and Paul in his greeting to the church at Rome and his letter to the church at Corinth. This needed to be added because the chapter added that section but doesn't call it out here.

## Jesus Revealed Himself

Looking at Scripture as the foundation of any theological belief, we look first to Jesus. In Luke 24:13–27, the biblical account describes Jesus and two of his disciples on the road to Emmaus. This story is rich in theology. In this passage, Luke shows the ubiquity of Christ woven throughout Scripture. Furthermore, we can see how Jesus' teachings consistently employed Old Testament Scripture to bear witness to his life and ministry and to reinforce

1. Stott, *God's Word*, 16.

the weight of his mission.[2] Through this passage, I hope to show that each text of Scripture reveals a gospel connection within its grammatical-historical, Christocentric hermeneutic.

Before we go too far, there is one thing worth noting. There is a historical debate about the location of Emmaus and, therefore, about the distance the disciples travelled between Jerusalem and the town. The discussion about Emmaus's location has left its location uncertain. Even by Eusebius and Jerome, the church fathers had already confused the city, only adding to the long-held uncertainty.[3] This disagreement is an essential point because the consensus on the distance is between seven and eighteen miles. Let us not be naïve to assume ignorance here. Whatever the estimation, one thing is clear. The time to travel the distance is insufficient to cover the whole of Scripture. Luke's account employs hyperbole to convey the Old Testament significance of the death, burial, and resurrection of Jesus Christ throughout Scripture. This rhetorical approach establishes the whole from its contingent parts. For example, if we take a wall and assert that it is such, then we can examine a single brick in the wall to establish the key characteristics of the wall's overall composition. By examining the bricks, we can infer the wall's characteristics. This same principle applies to the inference of the ubiquity of Christ.

Moreover, this is in keeping with Luke's writing style; the Emmaus narrative demonstrates the architecture of Scripture's story and Luke's literary artistry.[4] Luke attests to the weaving of Christ's message throughout the Old Testament. This Christocentric thread is evident in his use of the phrase "beginning with Moses and with all the prophets" (Luke 24:27). What is more, the word *all* appears three times in verses 25–27.[5] This point stresses the whole nature of Jesus, proving that his messianic fulfilment was comprehensive. We can see Luke's use of hyperbole in Luke 24:27 to reinforce the greater implication of his argument; there is Old Testament evidence of the person and work of Christ. Here are three points of consideration from this text.

2. Stott, *God's Word*, 14.

3. Lange and van Oosterzee, *Luke*, 391.

4. Carroll, *Luke*, 482.

5. Osborne, *Luke*, 570.

### *Jesus Corrects His Disciples*

There is an old proverb that goes, "Familiarity breeds contempt"—the notion that excessive knowledge or association with something leads to a loss of respect for it. Maybe we find that passive attitude here with Jesus' disciples. He chides them for their—and, dare I say, our—edification. Here, Jesus appears to them concealed, hears their story, and ultimately identifies their disregard for the Old Testament. Once they had shared the events of the day with Jesus, Jesus responded.

In Luke 24:25, Jesus' response is to further explain the events to the disciples. Theologian H. D. M. Spence attested that the disciples' story was confusing, and Jesus scolded them in response.[6] Jesus' exclamation shows us the intense emotion with which Jesus responded. This passionate response is consistent throughout New Testament passages (Mark 9:19, Luke 9:41, Acts 13:10, Gal 3:1).[7] It does not necessarily mean that Jesus was yelling. I do not see, within the context of the text, anything that would indicate that. Instead, he speaks with passion. I imagine the same way you strike a chord in conversation with someone: revealing their passion. Their tone, demeanor, and inflection resound with passion for the subject at hand. Have a conversation with me about Scripture or hermeneutics, and I will light up (and quite possibly ramble on for hours). I believe that the text indicates a passion for the mission at hand. Jesus' mission was to obey the Father and seek and save the lost. I can see Jesus in this narrative, teaching with passionate correction for their lack of understanding, but ultimately for their good and for the good of the gospel.

The correction is evident in Jesus' use of the phrase "foolish men" (v. 25). J. C. Ryle stated, "Here it only means 'wanting in thought, understanding, and consideration,' and does not imply any contempt."[8] This phrase is not intended to relegate them as unbelievers but rather to demonstrate their ignorance of the subject to which they have espoused expertise. When Jesus approached them, they asked, "Are you the only one visiting Jerusalem and unaware of the things which have happened here in these days" (Luke 24:18). They recounted the events of the death of Jesus with authority. Nevertheless, they were ignorant of the actual mystery that had unfolded.

6. Spence, *Gospel According to Luke*, 271.

7. Marshall, *Gospel of Luke*, 891.

8. Ryle, *Luke*, 505.

Furthermore, Jesus' use and order of "foolish men" and "slow of heart" (v. 25) serves to indicate the metaphorical nature which Jesus intended.[9] This understanding considers the coordinating function of the conjunction *and*, as well as its equality in conjoining.[10] That is, consistently in the New Testament authorship, the former must match the latter in the use of *and*. Therefore, they are not literally opposed to God, nor are their hearts literally beating more slowly. The accusation is that they are slow to respond to the resurrection's spiritual truth. Jesus' phrasing stands as an emphatic assertion of their dismissal of Old Testament references to the Messiah, rather than the testimony of the women of Christ's resurrection and the attestation of the disciples returning from the empty tomb—the confirmation of Christ as foretold by the prophets. Christ saw their belief, but their faith was one-sided. Here, he offers a rebuke and stinging charge of their misunderstanding.

### *Jesus Instructs His Disciples*

In the same breath, Jesus then corrects their understanding, pointing to the truth of the necessity of his suffering and glorification. Verse 25 serves as the thematic summary that leads to one of the chapter's main emphases: the prophets have spoken![11] If verse 25 is the main thrust pointing back to the Old Testament, then verse 26 emphasizes Jesus' connection. Specifically, the central question in verse 26 is what connects the Old Testament to the events of the passion.[12] The text contains a chiasm in the narrative (Luke 24:25–27) that affirms the disciples' ignorance of the Old Testament, the necessity of Christ's suffering, and the Old Testament's explanation of it.

Jesus explained how his death, burial, resurrection, and glorification fulfilled Old Testament prophecies. Luke's use of the word *all* has two possible meanings: either he used the law and the prophets, or he searched all of Scripture, starting with the law and the prophets.[13] Essentially, it is the use of hyperbole as a rhetorical device that emphasizes the enormity of Christ's revelation in the Old Testament. Jesus' teaching on the entirety of the Old Testament would be impossible to cover in such a short distance. Therefore,

9. Reiling and Swellengrebel, *Gospel of Luke*, 754.
10. Heckert, *Discourse Function of Conjoiners*, 74.
11. Stein, *Luke*, 614.
12. Green, *Gospel of Luke*, 848.
13. Marshall, *Gospel of Luke*, 897.

it is safe to interpret Luke's statement as hyperbolic. Robert Stein stated, "The term 'all' is another example of Luke's fondness for exaggeration, for the time would not have permitted Jesus to refer to 'all' the Scriptures that referred to him."[14] However, Luke's assertion is significant, and we must not take it lightly. He was drawing out the point that Scripture reveals Jesus throughout itself. Ultimately, Jesus chose the passages regarded as "messianic" and showed how they should be understood.[15]

Moreover, Jesus demonstrated the necessity of all that had occurred. His use of the word *suffer* encompasses the whole of his sacrifice. The necessity of suffering encompassed his experience of rejection and death by crucifixion.[16] By drawing on Old Testament passages, Jesus is correcting the disciples' understanding of the Messiah's work. The disciples understood this in connection to Jerusalem—a promise reinterpreted. Graeme Goldsworthy wrote, "The content of this gospel message that Jesus preached consists of two main elements, that of certain expectations that are now fulfilled, and the approach of the kingdom of God. Both elements are saturated with the salvation history of the Old Testament message."[17]

Furthermore, Jesus' use of "enter into his glory" evokes remembrance of the transfiguration account (Luke 9:32) as well as the eschatological reference to exaltation (Luke 9:26). Carroll identified this declaration as a "divine answer" to the "repudiation" of human powers.[18] The shame and disdain Christ endured on the cross have now been made right through the exaltation of Christ's authority over death and the grave. Christ and his authority over death and the grave establish his eternal kingdom, and at the heart of his kingdom is the Christian community—the church—which he propagates by his life.[19] Ultimately, he demonstrated the splendor of God's sovereignty by vanquishing his enemies (Ps 110:1, Luke 20:42–43). Jesus' confirmation of the focal message of Scripture illuminates the Messiah and offers hope for believers' futures (1 Cor 5:15). Jesus corrected their understanding to show who he is and why he had to suffer. As a good rabbi would, he corrected their misconceptions and used Scripture to display the truthfulness of his claims.

14. Stein, *Luke*, 615.
15. Marshall, *Gospel of Luke*, 897.
16. Carroll, *Luke*, 485.
17. Goldsworthy, *Preaching the Whole Bible*, 95.
18. Carroll, *Luke*, 485.
19. Barton and Muddiman, *The Oxford Bible Commentary*, 958.

### *Jesus Compels His Disciples*

In Luke 24:13–27, Jesus unveils the truth of his redemptive work as foretold "beginning with Moses and with all the prophets" (v. 27). The crux of Jesus' argument rests on verses 25–26. Nevertheless, he explained the truth of his purpose through the Old Testament. He showed the disciples how to find the connection to his redemptive work woven throughout Scripture. Essentially, in recounting the Emmaus journey, Luke demonstrated the ubiquity of Christ as revealed throughout Scripture. Randy Newman stated,

> In the Scriptures, it all centers on the radical claims Jesus made about himself. He claimed to be one with the Father, a claim of deity (John 10:30–31). He said he was alive before the creation of the world, when "Satan [fell] like lightning from heaven" (Luke 10:18)—a bizarre delusion of grandeur if that's not the truth. And he said he'd still be with his disciples "always, to the very end of the age" (Matthew 28:20).[20]

Newman astutely drew upon Jesus' consistent truth claims regarding who he was, often grounded in the Old Testament. Luke further connects it, declaring that the whole of the Old Testament reveals Christ.

The road to Emmaus story concludes with an implicit call for response in three reflections. First, Jesus showed the necessity of the transformative power of truth. He lived out John 17:17, sanctifying his disciples through the word of truth. He unraveled the mystery in his disciples' minds using the God-breathed word recorded in the Old Testament. Conceptually, we will unpack this more in chapter 6, which I identify as a call to the mind.

Second, Luke asserted that the disciples, upon learning Jesus' identity, declared that their "hearts were burning" within them (v. 32) as the Lord taught them. I. Howard Marshall concluded of the disciples' experience that "believers may be able to recognize their inward warmth of heart as springing from the presence of the risen Lord."[21] The illumination of the truth of the word of God by Jesus comforts and invigorates them. The call is toward an inward reinvigoration of passion toward Christ. We will discuss this in more detail in chapter 6: how this is a call to the emotions.

Third, there is an impact of the truth on their minds and the power of the word upon their hearts. This impact compels them, despite their pleas with Jesus to stay because "the day is nearly over" (v. 29) to take up the road

20. Newman, *Mere Evangelism*, 70.

21. Marshall, *Gospel of Luke*, 899.

again. They set out "that very hour" (v. 33) to embark on a journey back to Jerusalem, intent on their purpose to bear witness to the eleven disciples that Christ was risen indeed. Again, we will discuss this in more detail in chapter 6: how this is a call to the volition or will. But more on these later.

### *Implications*

As Luke recounted, Jesus identified himself in the Old Testament, and we can hold to the truth that the person and work of Christ are revealed throughout Scripture (Old and New Testaments). John Stott noted, "Scripture is the Father's testimony to the Son. It points to him. It says to us, 'Go to him in order to find life—abundant life—in him.' Therefore, any preoccupation with the biblical text, which does not lead to a stronger commitment to Jesus Christ in faith, love, worship, and obedience, is seriously perverted."[22] The revelation of Christ in the Old Testament moves the disciples from despair to hope, first in their understanding and knowledge of Christ and then in their recognition of their emotional transformation. This transformation of seeing Christ moved them to action. Against the better judgment of the advice they had given Christ, they were compelled to bear witness with urgency. They returned that very hour!

## Philip and the Ethiopian

In addition to the road to Emmaus, I. Howard Marshall identified that there is an "exquisite comparison" to the Ethiopian eunuch (Acts 8:26–40) about revealing Christ in the journey, ignorance of Scripture, the illumination of Christ from the Old Testament, the supplication of the interpreter to stay, and disappearance.[23] This story, although brief, shows the apostles' deep seated conviction in the revelation of Jesus Christ from the Old Testament. It was the Lord's supernatural guidance that birthed this conviction.

The context of this narrative seems out of place. Before this section, we find the persecution of the church in Jerusalem. Following this section, we see Saul's conversion. Nevertheless, here we find an obscure passage about Philip and a seemingly random encounter with an Ethiopian. This section is vitally important in the context of Acts for at least the following

22. Stott, *God's Word*, 22.

23. Marshall, *Gospel of Luke*, 890.

two reasons. First, it demonstrates the fulfillment of, what could be argued, the single greatest verse in Acts—Jesus said, "But you will receive power when the Holy Spirit has come upon you; and you shall be My witnesses both in Jerusalem, and in all Judea and Samaria, and even to the remotest part of the earth" (Acts 1:8). John Polhill asserted, "The 'restoration of the kingdom' involves a worldwide mission. Jesus promised the disciples two things: power and witness."[24] This story is the first account of transcending the cultural boundaries into the gentile population. It comes with both the witness of Christ and the demonstrable power of the Holy Spirit.

Second, it shows the significance of God's providential hand at work in the early church. Persecution was beginning to erupt in Jerusalem, seemingly forcing the disciples to disperse (v. 4). As they dispersed, they preached the gospel. Grant Osborne wrote, "The Spirit once again takes over. An angel guided Philip in verse 26, showing the importance of this encounter, as all heaven is involved."[25] Between the fulfillment of Christ's own words and the providential move of God, this story falls where it does to illustrate these very points—the cross-cultural fulfillment of the gospel and the providence of God's plan.

### *Conviction Toward God*

Philip came up to the Ethiopian in his chariot. It is important to note that although the Ethiopian was a "God-fearing" gentile, he would have been limited in full conversion and membership in the community of Judaism because he was a eunuch (Deut 23:1). The fact that he was traveling to Jerusalem "to worship" demonstrates the resolve of his faith in God. Imagine the passion toward a belief system that would hold you at arm's length. Moreover, despite his conviction, he was unable to comprehend what he read from the scroll of Isaiah. Another way of looking at this is that the Ethiopian was convinced in his heart that the God of Jacob was the true God. The providence of God worked on the heart of the Ethiopian to receive the gospel. It is vitally important to see that the Holy Spirit guided Philip to this encounter. We can infer that, as the Holy Spirit led Philip, it is not a stretch to assert that the Holy Spirit was also leading the Ethiopian. The reach of the gospel begins to unfold through this story. The Ethiopian marks the beginning of the "ends of the earth" described in Acts 1:8.

24. Polhill, *Acts*, 86.

25. Osborne, *Acts*, 167.

### *Clarity of Christ from Isaiah*

Philip then shows the Ethiopian the meaning of Christ behind the passage in Isaiah. Isaiah 53:7–8 speaks to the suffering servant, death, and the penal substitution. Moreover, Polhill provided an exceptional analysis of this section. He wrote,

> The picture of the slaughtered lamb evokes the image of Jesus' crucifixion, the lamb before his shearers, that of Jesus' silence before his accusers. The deprivation of justice reminds one of the false accusations of blasphemy leveled at Christ and the equivocation of Pilate. But what does "who can speak of his descendants?" mean—that his life was cut off short or perhaps the opposite, that the tragedy of his death had been followed by a whole host of disciples who had come to believe and trust in him? In addition to the silent suffering and humiliation, the question concerning descendants likely was a point of identification that attracted the eunuch to this text. There is no question what the final phrase would mean to a Christian like Philip. When Christ's life was taken from the earth, it was taken up in the glory of the resurrection, exalted to the right hand of God.[26]

Philip's explanation of Isa 53 is not detailed but rather summed up: "Beginning from this Scripture he preached Jesus to him" (Acts 8:35). The implication is that it was not merely this verse that Philip employed. The particulars of how Philip showed Jesus in his outline of Scripture are missing, but the truth that he showed the Ethiopian Jesus from Isaiah is certain. Osborne revealed, "The idea of atonement procured is not emphasized (it is in 53:5–6) but is still in keeping with Isaiah 53 and so implicit here. This Servant is God's own agent and yet suffered an unjust death inflicted by a wicked generation."[27] The theme of the suffering of Jesus that ushered in the need for repentance, forgiveness of sins, and salvation—the gospel.

### *Immediacy of Response*

The completeness of the gospel message is on full display with the response to the Ethiopian's request for baptism. Implicit in the text is Philip's description of the necessity of faith in Christ and response in baptism. The

26. Polhill, *Acts*, 225.

27. Osborne, *Acts*, 167–68.

necessity of baptism as the Christian rite that followed conversion is present in the Ethiopian's response, "Look! Water! What prevents me from being baptized?" (v. 36). The urgency of profession demonstrated by the Ethiopian speaks to the immediacy of his reception of the gospel. The message of the gospel reveals that the barriers that prevented the Ethiopian from full membership in Judaism have been removed. He can, and does, become a baptized and fully devoted follower of Christ. Moreover, the Holy Spirit's movement is woven throughout the narrative. Polhill wrote, "The coincidences are too numerous to be coincidences. The Spirit was in *all* of this."[28]

### *Implications*

Several critical theological themes regarding the ubiquity of Christ in Scripture arise from this narrative. First, there exists a christological connection to the Old Testament. That Philip was able to present the gospel from the beginning, as seen in the passage from Isaiah, further confirms that. Second, the universal reach of the gospel is on full display. Where the Ethiopian was limited in his pursuit of God under Judaism, he now has unfettered access to the throne of grace through Jesus Christ. Finally, Philip's anchoring of the gospel message in Isaiah demonstrates the redemptive nature of Scripture. The unified message of Scripture reveals the redemptive implication within the revelation of Christ.

## Paul's Charge to the Romans

Paul's salutation to the church at Rome (Rom 1:1–7) enriches our understanding of Paul's foundational theology. The letter to the Romans does not command or negate Paul's theological treatise. It is essential to note the deep connection Paul draws out between the law of Moses and the new covenant. Douglas Moo wrote, "Because the law is central to the Mosaic covenant, Paul's discussion of the law becomes a discussion of the Mosaic covenant and its relationship to the New Covenant initiated in Christ."[29]

28. Polhill, *Acts*, 226.

29. Moo, *Letter to the Romans*, 25.

### *The Message Paul Proclaims*

Paul argued that God called him to proclaim the gospel. Moreover, it was God who had promised the gospel through his prophets in the Holy Scriptures. Paul is bringing about an understanding of the continuity between the Old and New Testaments. By grounding his message in the Old Testament Scriptures, Paul connects the *euangelion* to the long history of God's dealings with Israel. Matthew Queen attested that the classical Greek understanding of *euangelion* conveys a sense of reward for the message.[30] Lewis Drummond unpacks *euangelion* as meaning "reward for good news."[31] He asserted several significant truths that are part of the makeup of the gospel—the gospel brings salvation, the kingdom of God, immortality, affliction, truth, grace, peace, labor, responsibility, and ultimately God.[32] This understanding of the gospel aligns with Paul's connection to the Mosaic law and with the result of obedience, as opposed to the result of the *euangelion*—salvation. Moo noted the ambiguity with which Paul often employs the word *euangelion*, yet concluded, "In saying that he has been 'set apart for the gospel of God' then, Paul is claiming that his life is totally dedicated to God's act of salvation in Christ."[33]

Paul then turns to the content of the gospel, focusing on Jesus Christ. He describes Jesus as descended from David, thus affirming Jesus' humanity and rightful place in the Davidic line. Paul illustrates how Jesus fulfilled the Jewish messianic expectations. He culminates in his gospel proclamation, declaring that Jesus is the Son of God. The resurrection attests to this message. Paul affirms Jesus' divinity and exalted status, demonstrated in power through his resurrection. The resurrection is a pivotal event that vindicates Jesus' identity and mission, inaugurating a new era in salvation history.

### *The Reward of the Gospel*

Paul explained his mission: to bring about the "obedience of faith" among all nations (v. 5). This phrase encapsulates Paul's understanding of the gospel's purpose—to produce a response of faith that leads to obedient living. To Paul, the gospel is not merely about intellectual assent but involves a

30. Queen, "Theological Assessment," 40.
31. Drummond, *Word of the Cross*, 205.
32. Drummond, *Word of the Cross*, 206.
33. Moo, *Letter to the Romans*, 41.

transformative obedience that flows from genuine faith. C. K. Barrett succinctly asserted, "The aim of Paul's apostleship is here defined as to win believing obedience."[34] Faith was sufficient to garner their acceptance into Christ. However, Paul fully understood that obedience is an expression of faith—the two are intertwined. Karl Barth wrote, "[Christ's] summons is, however, that they should give to him and therefore to God a true and serious and total faith: not a mere acceptance of the fact that he is their Lord nor an idle confidence that he helps them; but this acceptance and confidence as a faith that is lived out and practiced by them."[35]

Furthermore, the inclusion of nations (*ethnesin*) underscores the universal scope of Paul's mission and the gospel's relevance to all people, regardless of their ethnic or cultural background. Mounce attested, "The promised Messiah did not come for the benefit of the Jewish nation alone. The gospel is good news for all who will respond in faith."[36] According to Paul, faith resulted in obedience to Jesus as Lord. Osborne noted, "Evangelism was at the heart of Paul's gospel, but evangelism always leads to discipleship—to a Godward lifestyle. A truly New Testament church will be strong in both arenas—reaching the lost for Christ, and then enabling them to grow more deeply in their walk with Christ."[37]

Finally, in verses 6–7, Paul addresses the Roman Christians directly. He acknowledged that they are among those "called of Jesus Christ" (v. 6). This calling is both a privilege and a responsibility, signifying their identity as God's chosen people. Paul extends a greeting of "grace and peace" from God the Father and the Lord Jesus Christ, encapsulating the essence of the Christian message. The consistency of Paul's salutation ordering is theologically significant—the pairing of "grace" then "peace" consistently appears in that order in Pauline letters (1 Cor 1:3, 2 Cor 1:2, Gal 1:3, Eph 1:2, Phil 1:2, Col 1:2, 1 Thess 1:1, 2 Thess 1:2, 1 Titus 1:4, Phil 3) with only a slight variations in 1 Timothy and 2 Timothy. God's grace and unmerited favor precede peace with God due to reconciliation through Christ.

34. Barrett, *Epistle to the Romans*, 22.

35. Barth, *Call to Discipleship*, 16–17.

36. Mounce, *Romans*, 62.

37. Osborne, *Romans*, 24–25.

### *Implications*

Several key theological themes emerge from these verses. First, the continuity between the Old and New Testaments is evident as Paul roots his message in the prophetic promises of Scripture. Second, the dual nature of Jesus as both human and divine is emphasized, with the resurrection as the definitive proof of his divine sonship. Third, the "obedience of faith" concept highlights the ethical and transformative dimensions of the gospel. Finally, the universal scope of the gospel underscores God's inclusive plan of salvation for all people. Romans 1:1–7 serves as a powerful and theologically rich introduction to Paul's epistle, laying the foundation for the profound discussions that follow. It establishes Paul's authority, outlines the gospel message, and emphasizes the universal and transformative nature of God's salvation in Jesus Christ. Ultimately, the emphasis on "obedience of faith" illuminates the summons of Christ's preaching in Scripture.

## The Light Brought About by the Gospel

As we consider the ubiquity of Christ woven throughout Scripture, it is essential to examine both the theology and the example set by the apostles. Paul elevated the significance of the light brought about by the gospel in 2 Cor 4:3–6. The light of the gospel reveals the glory of God, and apart from Christ, there is spiritual blindness. Murray Harris noted, "Paul makes it clear that the reason for the 'veiledness' of the gospel in the case of those who are perishing (v. 3) is not the gospel itself (it brings enlightenment, v. 4b), nor himself as its agent, but the activity of Satan in blinding their minds to the truth of the gospel."[38]

In essence, the gospel of Jesus Christ reveals the glory of God to the hearts and minds held captive by Satan. What lies at stake in the discussion of the gospel of Jesus is this duality of understanding. To those perishing, the devil conceals the gospel because he has "blinded the minds of the unbelieving so that they might not see the light of the gospel of the glory of . . . Christ" (2 Cor 4:4). Rudolf Bultmann asserted, "What is at stake in the question of faith is the either-or, God or Satan. There is not a third thing between."[39] The light of the gospel illuminates the need. The gospel, then, is not about the strength and virtues of the believer but the person of Christ.

38. Harris, *Second Epistle to the Corinthians*, 327.

39. Bultmann, *Second Letter to the Corinthians*, 103.

It is Christ who strengthens the weak, gives sight to the blind, and frees the captive from the bondage of Satan.

### *Grounded in Creation*

Paul then established the foundational source of Christ's power. Just as God spoke light into existence, placing his glory on full display, so Christ illuminates the human heart through the gospel, enabling it to behold the glory of God. The significance of the light of the gospel message rests firmly in this creation connection. The light of the gospel of Jesus serves to establish within the heart of man the freedom to behold the glory of God. We can rightly draw parallels between John's notion of the light of Christ in the creation of the world (the Word espoused in John 1:1) and Paul's connection of the light of Christ in the new creation through the gospel.

First, we can see the intrinsic connection of the necessity of the word. The same God who, by his word, ushered all things into existence now brings new life into existence through the Word—Christ Jesus our Lord. Both demonstrate the glory of God through Christ Jesus. God's chosen means to create life (his words) turns out to be his chosen means to reveal new life through salvation (the Word). Both Paul and John illustrate God's self-disclosure through Christ—piercing the darkness and spiritual blindness. In both instances, the word is the agent of creation. The same divine word that brought the physical into existence now compels people to new life through the gospel.

Second, we can see the connection between light and divine revelation. Both Paul and John point to Jesus as the light of creation, grounding the person and work of Christ (the gospel) in the beginning revealed in Gen 1. In the first creation, light illuminated God's glory through all he would do. In the new creation, the light breaks the bonds of captivity, illuminating God's glory in what he has done. The word spoken brings illumination, first to the universe and then to the heart of man. From that illumination comes life. The very existence of mankind is a direct result of God speaking. Incidentally, the same truth can be asserted about the spiritual state of man. The gospel proclaimed brings life through the illumination of Christ—more on that in chapter 5. Where John established the divinity and preexistence of Christ anchored in creation, Paul turns the conversation to the spiritual renewal that takes place in the new creation through Christ. The essence of these passages is that it is Christ himself who reveals the glory of God, overcomes the darkness to give life, and brings new life to those who believe.

## Conclusion

Considering the ubiquity of Christ in Scripture, the expectation of responding to Christ is implicit—the summons of the text toward salvation through justification and sanctification. We must strive to seek out Christ in the Scriptures in his right context. Throughout the Bible, Jesus is revealed and offers hope and redemption. Apart from the transformative message of the gospel, we are left with moral platitudes. It is in the person and work of Christ that we find lasting change by the power of the Holy Spirit. From Genesis to Revelation, the message of Christ is woven throughout Scripture and ultimately resonates with his glory. The ubiquity of Christ is not merely some theological overlay. Rather, it is the very fabric of the revelation of Scripture. This christological perspective asserts that the central theme of Scripture is the revelation of God's character and nature—expressed in the person and work of Jesus Christ. Alistair Begg succinctly stated, "We find Christ in all the Scriptures. In the Old Testament, he is predicted, in the Gospels he is revealed, in Acts he is preached, in the epistles he is explained, and in Revelation he is expected."[40] Preaching goes beyond the self-help persuasion. Preaching is the preacher's participation in the continual renewal process anchored in Scripture. Just as God has spoken, we must be willing to listen. Just as his words were written, we must strive toward faithful understanding. Just as we proclaim God's word, it speaks, and we must obey and conform to the response it calls us to make—its summons. Scripture issues a call, compels a charge, and there is an expectation of a response.

40. Begg, *Preaching for God's Glory*, 36.

# CHAPTER 4

# Preaching Christ from Scripture

In the previous chapter, we established that the thread of Christ's message runs through the whole of Scripture, that nestled within the main idea of each thought in Scripture lies a connection—whether explicit or implicit—to the person and work of Christ. This chapter aims to understand how the apostles would have understood this and how they would have established Christ as the central theme of their gospel. Essentially, since Christ is woven in Scripture, then preach Jesus from every Scripture. The preaching of the New Testament apostles is referred to as the primitive (or apostolic) *kerygma*, and its meaning is hotly contested. As such, it will serve our conversation well to address the historical views of the kerygma and to clarify my meaning moving forward.

For those of you who are unfamiliar with the kerygma, it stands as a core component of early Christian preaching, focusing on the life, death, resurrection, and exaltation of Jesus Christ (Acts 2:14–36, 1 Cor 15:1–8). Central to the kerygma is the announcement of Jesus' resurrection, scriptural evidence, and the call to repentance.[1] This proclamation confronts listeners with the reality of God's intervention in history and invites them to reconsider their beliefs and values. Repentance and faith are often presented as precursors to entering the kingdom of God in the call to respond to the kerygma.[2] It is not a purely intellectual one but rather one of personal and communal transformation, and therefore must be accompanied by an intentional response.[3] Scripture records the message as coupled with

1. Queen, *Recapturing Evangelism*, 107.
2. Drummond, *Word of the Cross*, 275.
3. Stewart, *Faith to Proclaim*, 116.

baptism, and the infilling of the Holy Spirit that empowers believers for new life and witness (Acts 2:38). The response Peter called for is obedience in the faith of the mind and the volition of the body. Preaching the gospel rests in pleading for restoration with God, which is accomplished through divine transformation of the heart, culminating in correct behavior.[4] Thus, the kerygma culminates in a call to the mind, the will, and the emotions of the whole person to repentance, faith, and obedience in discipleship (2 Tim 3:16, 4:2). Peter ultimately invited his audience into a transformative relationship with Jesus Christ and his kingdom community.

## Historic Views of the Apostolic Kerygma

*Kerusso* is the Greek word commonly translated as "preaching." In theology, the term *kerygma* became synonymous with the proclamation of the gospel. The debate over kerygma in scholarship centers on ascertaining the core message of Christianity and the resulting essence of apostolic preaching. Beginning in the twentieth century, with C. H. Dodd, scholarship set out to understand what the apostles held to be the primitive kerygma.[5] The kerygma encapsulates essential truths about Jesus Christ communicated by the apostles—his death, resurrection, and the promise of his return. However, a great debate grew around what constituted the apostolic message. Over the years, discussion and diversity have arisen around what the apostles proclaimed. The core understanding of how the apostles handled the proclamation of Christ (as seen in these historical views of the kerygma) offers varying hermeneutical approaches.[6] These theological positions led to the categorization of the kerygma into three primary schools—the British School of Kerygmatic Interpretation, the German School of Kerygmatic Interpretation, and the Anglican School of Kerygmatic Interpretation. The theological understanding of the summons warrants a basic overview of these schools. The various interpretive schools' approaches to the kerygma, consequently, influence how we view the early church's missional and evangelistic methodology. An introductory examination of the kerygmatic interpretive schools addresses these implications.

4. Smith, *Preaching for a Verdict*, 96.
5. Poe, *Gospel and Its Meaning*, 20.
6. Queen, *Recapturing Evangelism*, 103–4.

### *British School of Kerygmatic Interpretation*

First, the British School of Kerygmatic Interpretation—hereafter the British School—arose from the research of C. H. Dodd, a British theologian and professor specializing in textual criticism and exegesis at the University of Cambridge. In *The Apostolic Preaching and Its Developments*, Dodd laid the foundational groundwork for the content of the kerygma. He contended that there existed a distinction between the New Testament writer's understanding of teaching (*didache*) and preaching (*kerygma*). Dodd asserted, "It was by *kerygma*, says Paul, and not by *didache* that it pleased God to save men."[7] In his understanding, the kerygma was not the "action of the preacher, but that which he preaches."[8] Under this definition, the content of what we preach sets the core of the kerygma.

Moreover, Dodd articulated six essential components of the kerygma: (1) the age of messianic fulfillment has arrived; (2) the new era has come to pass through the death, burial, and resurrection of Jesus Christ; (3) the Father exalted Christ to his right hand through the resurrection; (4) the Holy Spirit is a sign within the church of Christ's power and glory; (5) the consummation of the messianic age will be Christ's return; and (6) the kerygma effectively closes with an appeal for repentance.[9] Dodd, therefore, offered up a creedal formulation of the kerygma in what he called the "Pauline kerygma" (where he examined Paul's proclamation) and the "Jerusalem kerygma" (where he examined Peter's proclamation). His analysis of the kerygma aids modern scholars' understanding of the early Christian message and its emphasis on the transformative power of Jesus Christ's life, death, and resurrection. It is vital to note that the British School explicitly asserted the connection between the appeal and the kerygma.

Additionally, James Stewart—a Scottish theologian who served as professor of New Testament language, literature, and theology at the University of Edinburgh—expounded on Dodd's work in his book *A Faith to Proclaim*. This book examined the early church kerygma, closely following the outline Dodd provided.[10] Stewart contended, "They proclaimed that prophecy was fulfilled; that in Jesus of Nazareth, His words and deeds, His life and death and resurrection, the new age had arrived; that God had exalted Him,

7. Dodd, *Apostolic Preaching*, 8.
8. Dodd, *Apostolic Preaching*, 1.
9. Dodd, *Apostolic Preaching*, 24–28.
10. Stewart, *Faith to Proclaim*, 29.

that He would come again as Judge and that now was the day of salvation."[11] He identified five components of early church kerygma: the incarnation of Christ, forgiveness being available, an emphasis on the cross, the resurrection as a distinct component, and the promise of a relationship with Christ. However, Stewart—unlike Dodd—emphasized the more practical and pastoral aim of blending content with a passionate delivery of the gospel, thereby integrating theological truths with practical emphasis.[12] The aim of the kerygma was "not for the propagating of views, opinions, and ideals" but for "the proclamation of the mighty acts of God."[13] For Stewart, the practical aim of the sermon was the balance between the indicative and the imperative—the declaration of truth and the call to respond to that truth—with the emphasis first on what Christ has done before what he expects.[14]

The British School provides a clear connection to the biblical expectation that the hearer respond to the message proclaimed. Carl Bradford elucidated, "A distinctive feature of the British School's understanding of the *kerygma* lies within the emphasis on content."[15] This content is the basis for the call to respond to the message proclaimed. The content of the kerygma of the British School rests upon the person and work of the historical Jesus. Overall, the British School's emphasis on the content lends itself to understanding the summons of the message within the kerygma—in an almost creedal fashion.

### *German School of Kerygmatic Interpretation*

The German School of Kerygmatic Interpretation—hereafter, the German School—arose from the history of understanding the interpretive difference between *historisch* and *geschichtlich*, the German words that translate as "history." For the German School, *historisch* refers to the facts of occurrence used for impartial analysis, while *geschichtlich* refers to history seen through philosophical or theological interpretation.[16] The foundation of *historisch* and *geschichtlich* lies within the German existential hermeneutic.

11. Stewart, *Faith to Proclaim*, 14–15.
12. Stewart, *Faith to Proclaim*, 34–35.
13. Stewart, *Heralds of God*, 5.
14. Stewart, *Heralds of God*, 154.
15. Bradford, "Schooling the Gospel," 21.
16. Congdon, *Rudolf Bultmann*, 90.

The German Enlightenment sought to ground the interpretation of the New Testament in neutral historical analysis.

The German School sought to establish the *historisch* of the New Testament and to capture the existential nature of the kerygma, which is dependent upon *geschichtlich*. This approach flows from Rudolf Bultmann's work *Kerygma and Myth*. Bultmann, a German theologian and professor of New Testament at the University of Marburg, specialized in demythologizing the New Testament, which led to existential interpretation. He held that faith in the proclamation of the gospel was not dependent upon a historical Jesus. Bultmann contended that the haecceity, not the quiddity, was the essence of belief in the kerygma.[17]

For Bultmann, the haecceity identifies the uniqueness of the gospel message—Jesus' existence, preaching, and death by crucifixion—that matters. He discounted the quiddity of the kerygma, identifying only the specific aspects of form that made it common among the apostles. Bultmann asserted,

> The message of Jesus is a presupposition for the theology of the New Testament rather than a part of that theology itself. For New Testament theology consists in the unfolding of those ideas employing which the Christian faith makes sure of its own object, basis, and consequences. But Christian faith did not exist until there was a Christian *kerygma*, i.e., a *kerygma* proclaiming Jesus Christ—specifically Jesus Christ the Crucified and Risen One—to be God's eschatological act of salvation. He was first so proclaimed in the *kerygma* of the earliest church, not in the message of the historical Jesus.[18]

His argument was rooted in his *a posteriori* focus of the first-century church—the proclamation of the message from their experiences. Bultmann was less concerned with the systematized description of the kerygma and more interested in the existential importance of understanding. He attempted to decouple the historical aspects of the Bible from what he deemed Christian mythology, including the virgin birth, the miracles of Jesus' ministry, and even the resurrection itself. Bradford summarized that the German School's emphasis is on "a mystical existential aspect of Christ"

17. The haecceity refers to aspects of a thing that make it a particular thing—its "thisness" or uniqueness. Quiddity refers to the universal qualities that make a thing—its "thatness" or commonality. For further reading on haecceity and quiddity, see Wilkens, *Christian Ethics*.

18. Bultmann, *Theology of the New Testament*, 3.

and that "the events [of Christ], although historical, serve as a channel for experiencing Christ."[19] Bultmann considered the proclamation of the kerygma a language event—a *Sprachereignis* (language event) in the Martin Heidegger sense.[20] The essence of the kerygma resides in the language event of its proclamation. David Congdon stated, "The *kerygma* proclaims the Christ-event, and in the act of proclamation, it becomes the present actualization of the event."[21]

Building upon Bultmann was Hans Conzelmann, a German theologian and professor of the New Testament at the University of Göttingen. In *An Outline of the Theology of the New Testament*, he argued that to make Christianity relevant to the modern age, it must decouple the myths from the Bible and focus on humanity's existential questions. He stated, "No primitive Christian preaching has been transmitted to us,"[22] thereby arguing against the British School's understanding of the kerygma's content in favor of an existential approach. Regarding the presentation of the kerygma in the New Testament, he argued, "The sermons in the Acts of the Apostles are neither sermons which were really given nor exacts from them, but purely literary creations from the hand of Luke."[23] This conclusion suggests a lack of historical validity to the kerygma and further propelled the existential view espoused by Bultmann. Bradford stated, "Bultmann articulates the lack of confidence of the German School to accept the speeches of Acts as historically reliable."[24] Erring on the side of skepticism draws the natural implication of experience over content. Conzelmann contended that faith demonstrates the truthfulness of the resurrection, whereas historical evidence cannot.[25] Therefore, the lack of historical confidence leads to dependence on the language events of the authors' experience.

As a result, the German School holds that historians must objectively establish the events of Jesus' life—such as his ministry, death, and resurrection—otherwise they are myths. Bradford summarized the German School when he wrote, "The German School, whether intentionally or

19. Bradford, "Schooling the Gospel," 72–73.

20. For a fuller understanding of *sprachen ereignis* (language event) as espoused by Martin Heidegger, see his work *Being and Time*.

21. Congdon, *Rudolf Bultmann*, 69.

22. Conzelmann, *Theology of the New Testament*, 88.

23. Conzelmann, *Theology of the New Testament*, 89.

24. Bradford, "Schooling the Gospel," 77.

25. Conzelmann, *Theology of the New Testament*, 88.

unintentionally, separates the 'Christ of Faith' from Scripture."[26] The German School approaches the kerygma from the perspective of individual experience, drawing the hearer into the community of believers. Historical evidence is unconvincing to Bultmann and company. Thus, a greater understanding must be sought through proclamation. Therefore, according to the German School, the experience—encapsulated in the apostolic preaching event—constitutes the gospel and not the content of the message.

### *Pre-Anglican School of Kerygmatic Interpretation*

As the academic quest for the kerygma progressed, Michael Green, a British theologian and apologist, offered a voice of dissent against the traditionally held views of the British and German Schools. His contention with Dodd rested on Dodd's assertion of the fixed content of the kerygma.[27] Additionally, he contended that Bultmann and company narrowly focused on existential experience and neglected historical truths. Green pronounced, "Both positions tend to soft-pedal the evidence, which is inconvenient to them."[28]

Green critiqued the more rigid approaches to the kerygma, advocating for a balance between theological precision and the dynamic nature of evangelistic preaching. He argued, "There has been undue concentration on what has become technically known as the *kerygma*."[29] He posited that evangelism does not occur in a vacuum but with real people in real-world situations and, therefore, must be tailored to them in terms that make sense. Green sought to strike a balance by accepting the aspects of the British and German Schools that were verifiable from Scripture and rejecting the aspects that weakened their arguments.

Green's understanding of the kerygma emphasizes that it is not just a historical account but a definable, propositional body of theological truth about Jesus Christ. He asserted that the message of the early church was fundamental homogeneity. Green asserted that the apostles preached the person of Christ, salvation as the gift of the message proclaimed, and a call for a response from their hearers.[30] This perspective emphasizes the es-

26. Bradford, "Schooling the Gospel," 80.
27. Green, *Evangelism in the Early Church*, 92.
28. Green, *Evangelism in the Early Church*, 94.
29. Green, *Evangelism in the Early Church*, 48.
30. Green, *Evangelism in the Early Church*, 150–52.

sential message of salvation through Jesus Christ, focusing on themes such as God's love, human sin, Christ's death and resurrection, and the call to repentance and faith.

Additionally, Lewis Drummond, an American theologian and former professor of evangelism at the Southern Baptist Theological Seminary, declared that the British School argues for an essential and fundamental content. At the same time, the German School tends "to emphasize the existential, experiential elements of proclaiming Christ strongly."[31] He demonstrated that effectiveness in evangelism is deeply rooted in a commitment to biblical inerrancy and solid theology. He bridged that gap, showing that the kerygma had both cognitive and experiential aspects. The former included sound theological doctrines, while the latter focused on spiritual renewal and revival.

Regarding Green's understanding of the gospel, Drummond asserted, "It is clear [Green] also sees the essential proclamation as a definable, propositional body of theological truth concerning Jesus Christ."[32] He demonstrated that this proclamation should be communicated with conviction and clarity, reflecting the essence of the gospel's good news. His perspective highlights the importance of making the gospel relevant and understandable to contemporary audiences. Drummond emphasized that the kerygma should encompass cognitive and experiential elements.

First, the cognitive aspect must involve presenting theological truths about Christ—such as the authority of Scripture, salvation, the kingdom of God, and the Trinity. The written word (the Bible) differs from the living Word (Jesus), but the written word reveals the living Word. Drummond attested, "In the Holy Scriptures, God has delivered an authoritative, trustworthy, true, propositional revelation of Himself that stands the epistemological test of comprehensiveness, coherence, correspondence, noncontradiction, and experience."[33] Therefore, the cognitive theological understanding of the kerygma is rooted in the revelation of Christ in Scripture.

Second, the experiential aspect focuses on the spiritual renewal and revival that should accompany gospel proclamation. Drummond's belief in God's suprarational character and the importance of propositional revelation helped shape his approach to evangelism. He declared, "God's

31. Drummond, *Word of the Cross*, 214.

32. Drummond, "Build a Foundation."

33. Drummond, *Word of the Cross*, 62.

salvation is all-inclusive and all-encompassing. The total person is saved by God's fathomless grace."[34] The essence of salvation encompasses the whole self—the mind, the emotions, and the volition.[35] Drummond contended that, as such, salvation contains an aspect of experience—deliverance from sin, deliverance from self, deliverance from standing judgment.[36] Therefore, the experiential theological understanding of the kerygma is rooted in the revelation of Christ, leading to spiritual renewal. Drummond confidently asserted, "If God is in this mission enterprise—and he surely is—solutions and success can be found."[37]

Ultimately, Drummond illustrated the importance of balancing the existential experience and the content of the gospel proclamation, stating that the New Testament kerygma was more than "theological dogma" and required a "positive faith response."[38] Drummond argued, "[Understanding the kerygma] alone falls short of the whole story of effective proclamation. The proper spiritual dynamic is vital to the success of evangelistic declaration."[39] Therefore, at its most basic, the effective witness is a man or woman of God declaring his word. Summarizing his views on the kerygma, Drummond contended for two truths: "A biblical content rests at the core," and, "The full *kerygma* must be wisely contextualized."[40]

Furthering the conversation, Harry Poe, an American theologian and professor of faith and culture at Union University, proposed in *The Gospel and Its Meaning* that Dodd argued an artificial separation between *kerygma* and *didache*. His primary concern rested upon a whole view of the gospel encompassing Christ's proclamation and teaching. He asserted, "While Dodd's critics appear to be correct that the *kerygma* did not exist as a fixed formula, Dodd was correct to the extent that the *kerygma* existed as a fixed content upon which the early Christians drew when proclaiming their faith in Christ."[41] He struck at the heart of the tension between the British and

34. Drummond, *Word of the Cross*, 222.

35. This observation is in concert with the exegesis of 2 Tim 4:1–5. The gospel redeems our understanding of God, our affections of the heart toward God, and ultimately how we act in response to God.

36. Drummond, *Word of the Cross*, 225–29.

37. Drummond, *Reaching Generation Next*, 131.

38. Drummond, *Word of the Cross*, 204.

39. Drummond, *Word of the Cross*, 216.

40. Drummond, *Reaching Generation Next*, 85.

41. Poe, *Gospel and Its Meaning*, 44.

German Interpretive Schools—the opposed creed and the affirmed content. Poe argued, "The good news of Christ requires both the *kerygma* and the *didache*. The *kerygma* establishes Christ concretely as the decisive act of God for the salvation of the world. . . . The *didache* unfolds the significance of the *kerygma* for salvation."[42]

Poe stated that Jesus used Scripture to validate who he was while bringing the essence of the gospel through his life and teachings. He stated, "Jesus did not challenge the Jewish understanding of the nature of Scripture; rather, he challenged the contemporary interpretation."[43] He then argued that the gospel message's authority rests upon its fulfillment in Scripture. Poe contended that Jesus identified himself as one who fulfills Scripture.[44] Therein, according to Poe, lies the content of the message of the kerygma. However, he did not neglect the existential aspects of the German School. Poe wrote, "The apostles experienced salvation through faith in Jesus Christ. Because of their faith in him, they viewed reality in a new perspective oriented toward Christ, which they called repentance."[45]

Green and company demonstrated the value of examining the content while valuing the existential experience in the gospel proclamation. The kerygma results in a thorough call to transform the mind, emotions, and will—faith resulting in obedience. The consistent conclusion of the British and German Schools, as evidenced by Green and company, establishes the necessity of responding to Christ's message. Therefore, this intermediary view holds that the gospel renews every aspect of a person's life, affecting the mental, emotional, and physical states to draw him or her toward spiritual renewal.

### *Anglican School of Kerygmatic Interpretation*

The Anglican School of Kerygmatic Interpretation—hereafter the Anglican School—responded to the British and German Interpretive School's apparent overly *soterian* (salvation) approach to the modern understanding of the kerygma. Examining the concept broached by Green and company influenced the Anglican School's search for the grand narrative of Scripture concerning the social implications of the gospel under the kingship of

42. Poe, *Gospel and Its Meaning*, 45.
43. Poe, *Gospel and Its Meaning*, 81.
44. Poe, *Gospel and Its Meaning*, 85.
45. Poe, *Gospel and Its Meaning*, 290–91.

Christ. Bradford asserted, "The origin of the development [of the Anglican School] appeared to have its first signs with Michael Green's disagreement with both the British School and the German School and increased as the New Perspective and Contemporary scholars' investigations continued."[46] The Anglican School posits that the kerygma comprises the metanarrative story of redemption woven through Scripture, culminating in the kingship of Christ.

Scot McKnight—an American theologian and New Testament professor at Northern Baptist Theological Seminary—defined the kerygma as the proclamation of Scripture telling of the story of Jesus.[47] McKnight rejected salvation as a component of the kerygma but rather argued, "The word gospel has been hijacked by what we believe about 'personal salvation,' and the gospel itself has been reshaped to facilitate making 'decisions.'"[48] His conviction was to separate the proclamation of the gospel itself from the effect of the gospel proclamation—that is, the kingship of Christ as the fulfillment of Israel's story and the salvation of people. McKnight rightly argued that the *soterian* kerygma has emphasized the plan of salvation to the point of neglecting and losing the biblical gospel—the story of Israel and Jesus.[49] The focus on a salvation experience neglected the first-century Jewish understanding of the kerygma culmination of the new age of Christ's kingship. The necessity of the greater narrative of Scripture does not culminate in the salvation of men but in Christ's ascending the throne as King.

Building upon McKnight, N. T. Wright—an English theologian specializing in New Testament theology and a senior research fellow at the University of Oxford—argued that the gospel is not "how to have your sins forgiven" or "how to go to heaven."[50] Instead, he asserted that the Gospels show "how God became King—in and through Jesus. . . . The one who sits in heaven is the one who rules on earth."[51] Wright argued for the distinction in the message and disparity between the Gospels and the apostles' message. The former declared Christ to be King, but the latter emphasized that Jesus is God.[52] The essence of the Anglican School's argument rests upon

46. Bradford, "Schooling the Gospel," 157.

47. McKnight, *King Jesus Gospel*, 50.

48. McKnight, *King Jesus Gospel*, 26.

49. McKnight, *King Jesus Gospel*, 43.

50. Wright, *How God Became King*, 244.

51. Wright, *How God Became King*, 175.

52. Wright, *How God Became King*, 20.

Christ becoming King as the fulfillment of Israel's story and God's promise to Abraham.

Adding to the conversation, Matthew Bates—an American theologian specializing in the New Testament, early Christianity, and the gospel—challenged traditional views of faith by redefining it as allegiance to Jesus as King.[53] Bates asserted that salvation is not merely about intellectual belief or assent to doctrines but involves a dynamic, covenantal loyalty to Christ.[54] He posited that the "*pistis* [faith] as allegiance" includes "works as embodied allegiance."[55] He emphasized the gospel's climax in Jesus' ascension to the throne, calling for a shift from viewing faith as passive belief to active discipleship and commitment. This perspective reframes the gospel as a call to transformative allegiance, urging believers to embody their faith in tangible ways.

The Anglican view seeks to establish the apostolic gospel as the first-century church would have understood it. First, the gospel is the story of Jesus as the fulfillment of Israel's narrative. It further argues that the gospel is not merely a plan of salvation but the declaration of Jesus as the Messiah and Lord. Next, the gospel is the announcement of Jesus as the faithful Lord of the world, fulfilling God's covenant promises to Israel. This approach ties the gospel to the larger narrative of Scripture, focusing on God's kingdom breaking into the world through Jesus. Finally, the gospel is the proclamation of Jesus as King, calling for a response of loyalty and obedience. As a result, the Anglican view shares a commitment to a Christ-centered gospel, yet brings a distinct emphasis—the story of Jesus culminating in the kingdom and covenant that expects allegiance to Jesus as King.

## *The Theological Implications of the Apostolic Kerygma*

The kerygma is a cornerstone of early Christian theology with profound theological implications for a modern context. At its core, the kerygma encapsulates the essential message of the gospel as defined by Paul in 1 Cor 15—the life, death, resurrection, and exaltation of Jesus Christ.[56] As seen from the examination of the various interpretive schools, the proclamation is not merely a historical recounting of historical events in a quasi-credal

53. Bates, *Salvation by Allegiance Alone*, 4–5.

54. Bates, *Salvation by Allegiance Alone*, 99.

55. Bates, *Salvation by Allegiance Alone*, 110.

56. Dodd, *Apostolic Preaching*, 8–10.

form. Neither is it relegated to a theological affirmation of the transformation resulting from the gospel. The kerygma stands as the good news about the person and work of Jesus, the reward of that message played out in the response of the hearers, and the affirmation of God's redemption metanarrative throughout Scripture.

First, a central theological implication of the kerygma is the concept of salvation through Jesus Christ.[57] The apostles preached that Jesus' death and resurrection were pivotal events that offered redemption and reconciliation with God. The apostles' proclamation of the gospel emphasized that the law of Moses was insufficient for obtaining salvation. Instead, there was a need for faith in Jesus Christ as the Son of God and the Savior of the world. This understanding redefined the nature of God's covenant with humanity, emphasizing grace and faith over works.

Second, the kerygma highlights the eschatological dimension of the Christian faith.[58] The apostles proclaimed Jesus' resurrection as the firstfruits of a new creation and the harbinger of the final resurrection of the dead. This eschatological hope infused the early Christian community with a sense of urgency and expectation, as they believed the kingdom of God was at hand. The anticipation of Christ's return shaped their ethical and communal practices, encouraging a way of life that reflected the values of the kingdom to come.

Third, the kerygma stresses the universality of the gospel.[59] The apostles' proclamation broke down the barriers between Jews and gentiles, emphasizing that the message of salvation is for all people, regardless of ethnic or cultural background. Deep religious and ethnic divisions marked society in the first century, making this message revolutionary. The theological implication here is the idea of the church as a universal body of believers united in Christ and transcending all human divisions.

Fourth, the kerygma also asserts Jesus' authority as the exalted Lord.[60] Following his resurrection, God exalted Jesus to his right hand, signifying his divine authority and lordship over all creation. This affirmation of Jesus' divine status was fundamental to the apostolic message, as it called for a response of worship, obedience, and discipleship from the believers. Stewart wrote,

57. Drummond, *Word of the Cross*, 224.

58. Stewart, *Faith to Proclaim*, 30.

59. Green, *Evangelism in the Early Church*, 161.

60. Wright, *How God Became King*, 175.

> Thus, the apostolic preaching, which summoned men to behold God's glory in the past, and to await it in the future at the great Parousia, summoned them also to realize God's glory in the present moment. It is the present Lordship of Christ, inaugurated by His resurrection and exaltation to the right hand of God, that is the centre of the faith of primitive Christianity.[61]

The resurrection of Christ ushered in a fuller understanding of Christ's kingship as a present reality bookended by what was and will be. The acknowledgment of Jesus as Lord had profound implications for the identity and mission of the early church, as it rooted their faith and practice in the lordship of Christ.

The theological implications of the kerygma are vast and transformative. It defines salvation, infuses the faith with eschatological hope, asserts the universality of the gospel, and establishes the authority of Jesus Christ. These elements continue to shape Christian theology and practice, underscoring the enduring significance of the apostolic proclamation. However, analysis of these theological aspects reveals the necessity of original hearers to respond. R. Alan Streett illuminated that God speaks through his gospel "to the hearts," and to proclaim the kerygma devoid of the invitation is "disobedience to the Great Commission."[62]

The British School contended that the kerygma called for repentance from the hearers as part of its credal formulation of content.[63] The German Interpretive School held that responding to the kerygma was a call to personal transformation of authentic existence through the experience of the gospel proclamation.[64] Finally, the Anglican School concluded that the call to respond to the kerygma is to live out the reality of the resurrection as a sign of the kingship of Christ, in a way that impacts both personal faith and societal engagement.[65] Each school identified the necessity of a call for response—either as part of the kerygma or as a result of it. Therefore,

61. Stewart, *Faith to Proclaim*, 27.

62. Streett, *Effective Invitation*, 140.

63. For further reading on the British Interpretive School of Kerygmatic interpretation, see Dodd, *Apostolic Preaching*, and Stewart, *Faith to Proclaim*.

64. For further reading on the German Interpretive School of Kerygmatic interpretation, see Bultmann, *Theology of the New Testament*; Dibelius, *From Tradition to Gospel*; and Conzelmann, *Theology of the New Testament*.

65. For further understanding the Anglican Interpretive School of Kerygmatic interpretation, see Bock, *Recovering the Real Lost Gospel*; McKnight, *King Jesus Gospel*; Wright, *How God Became King*; Bates, *Salvation by Allegiance Alone*.

each interpretive school acknowledges the summons evidenced within the kerygma. By way of example, let us look to Peter as the first example in Acts of the kerygma.

## The Apostolic Preaching of Christ Culminating in a Summons

Within the passage of Act 2, we find the first gospel presentation recorded in the book of Acts. The occasion set forth rests on the proclamation following the miracle of the Holy Spirit at Pentecost. Darrell Bock stated, "This speech explains how the church presented its high Christology, something the event of Jesus's exaltation helped it to fully appreciate."[66] The transition beginning at verse 22 shifts from the apostles' defense against the accusation of being drunk to the defense of the divinity of Christ as Messiah and Lord. Peter examines Old Testament passages to reinforce the idea that the coming of the Holy Spirit fulfilled prophecy. Analyzing Peter's proclamation, F. F. Bruce espoused,

> The early Apostolic preaching regularly comprises four elements (not always in the same order): (1) the announcement that the age of fulfillment has arrived; (2) an account of the ministry, death, and triumph of Jesus; (3) citation of the Old Testament scriptures whose fulfillment in these events proves Jesus to be the one whom they pointed forward; (4) a call to repentance.[67]

The essence of Peter's proclamation rested on the resurrection as the ultimate and definitive divine confirmation of Jesus' nature as both Messiah and Lord. Peter boldly declared that the "last days" set forth by the prophet Joel (v. 16) now transition to the defense of Jesus' ministry. Marion Soards argued that Peter established a "christological kerygma" that encompasses how God attests to the crucifixion and is "actively expressive of the very will and work of God."[68]

John Polhill elucidated that the heart of Peter's proclamation rested in verses 22–36, through the declaration of "God's action in the ministry, death, and resurrection of Christ," drawing scriptural support from Pss 16

66. Bock, *Acts*, 118.

67. Bruce, *Book of the Acts*, 63.

68. Soards, *Speeches in Acts*, 33.

and 110.[69] Moreover, Marion Soards's analysis of the text reveals the shape of Peter's argument as a christological statement followed by a scriptural defense.[70] Polhill concurs with this assessment, identifying Christ's defense as Messiah in three parts: the argument for Christ's resurrection (vv. 22–28), the argument of Christ's lordship and messiahship (vv. 29–36), and the charge of the people and consequent call to respond (vv. 37–41).

### *Peter's Defense of Jesus' Resurrection*

For Peter's first argument and proof, he presented the claim that God raised Jesus by his power and plan (vv. 22–24). God attested through Jesus' demonstration of "miracles, signs, and wonders" during his earthly ministry.[71] F. F. Bruce contended that these "mighty works and wonders, and signs which God accomplished through Jesus of Nazareth" serve as God's sign of approval over the ministry and message of Jesus.[72]

However, Osborne elucidated Peter's connection between the crucifixion of Jesus by the Romans and the complicity of the Jews: "Peter skips over the life and ministry of Jesus, moving directly to his death. Peter emphasizes two things: that it was part of the divine plan and that the Jews, with the help of the 'wicked' Romans, were complicit in his death."[73] Peter provides the definitive judgment of man in contrast with God's supreme overruling power. Bruce drew a clear distinction that "the action of those who took part, directly or indirectly, in putting Jesus to death was overruled by God."[74] Therefore, no matter what man had set out to accomplish, God ultimately held their path and trajectory. For Peter, this fact alone was significant proof of Jesus' lordship and saviorship.

Next, Peter defends his position that Jesus is the Christ of God's plan by citing Ps 16:8–11 (Acts 2:25–28). Bock attested that Peter's use of the Old Testament served as a "typological-prophetic" proof of his confidence in God's attestation of Jesus.[75] Polhill asserted that the attribution to David

69. Polhill, *Acts*, 111.
70. Soards, *Speeches in Acts*, 33.
71. Polhill, *Acts*, 112.
72. Bruce, *Book of the Acts*, 63.
73. Osborne, *Acts*, 51.
74. Bruce, *Book of the Acts*, 64.
75. Bock, *Acts*, 123.

was crucial to Peter's argument for Jesus' "Davidic descent of the Messiah."[76] Soards noted the later use (Acts 13:35) with "a slightly different manner" but culminating in the "same point" as addressed here in his kerygma.[77] Primarily, the reverence of the first-century Jews for the Davidic line of kingship falls in the shadows of the cross and resurrection. Peter contended that, unlike David, who died and resides in his grave, God raised Christ from the dead, and he lives. Osborne noted, "Since David's body is still in the grave, Psalm 16's assertion of resurrection could not be about him. David's burial on Mount Zion is attested in 1 Kings 2:10, and to Peter, that means this prophecy is not about David but Christ."[78]

### *Peter's Defense of Jesus as Lord and Messiah*

For Peter's second argument and proof, he explains his confidence in Jesus as Lord and Messiah as evidenced in the resurrection (vv. 29–33). Soards declared, "David is cast as an authority on the Messiah here (2:25, 29, 34), in 4:25, and implicitly in 13:34–35."[79] This resurrection is central to Peter's message, affirming Jesus' identity as the Messiah. Bock attested, "Peter makes the explicit point that the resurrection indicates Jesus's position at the Father's right hand, as the one seated at God's side."[80] Furthermore, Peter explains that Jesus—not David—ascended to heaven and is now exalted at the right hand of God.[81] Also, because of Christ's ascension, the church has received the promised Holy Spirit from the Father. This Holy Spirit has been poured out upon the believers, as evidenced by the miraculous events occurring at Pentecost.

Finally, Peter's sermon concludes with (1) a declaration of confidence in the triumph of Jesus the Lord and Christ and (2) an assertion of the guilt of the crowd. Theologically, Peter's sermon declared the good news of the gospel—lordship and messiahship of Jesus—as painted upon the backdrop of its necessity—the guilt of the crowd. Soards demonstrated the significance of this coupling, which occurs in many speeches about Jesus.[82] Bock

76. Polhill, *Acts*, 114.
77. Soards, *Speeches in Acts*, 34.
78. Osborne, *Acts*, 53.
79. Soards, *Speeches in Acts*, 35.
80. Bock, *Acts*, 133.
81. Bruce, *Book of the Acts*, 67.
82. Soards, *Speeches in Acts*, 37.

rightly addressed that the ordering of verse 36 is of supreme importance: "The order of the Christological titles is important because 'Lord' is in the forward and emphatic position. It is the key title, as verses 21 and 34 connect it to the reference to Lord in Ps. 110:1 and Joel 3:5."[83] In addition, Bruce concluded, "But he has been exalted not only as Messiah and Son of God, but as Lord. The first apostolic sermon concludes with the first apostolic creed: 'Jesus is Lord.'"[84] Finally, the Christology of Jesus is at the heart of Peter's kerygma, which ultimately illuminates his lordship. Osborne wrote, "The movement from humiliation to exaltation and from Suffering Servant to triumphant Lord is at the heart of New Testament Christology."[85]

### *Call to Respond to the Gospel*

Historically, Peter's kerygma stands as an exemplar of effective evangelistic calls. Through the use of Scripture, reason, and dependence upon the Holy Spirit, Peter's sermon drew the crowd to conviction in both heart and mind. His call to respond from his audience had two significant components: the emotional impact of a sermon and a direct, concise appeal to respond.

First, the phrase "cut to the heart" (see v. 37) conveys the profound emotional and spiritual impact of Peter's sermon. Bock showed that this phrase demonstrates "the sincerity and depth of the audience's response."[86] William Willimon wrote, "Eventually, the gospel is about something for which there is no precedent—the resurrection—and we can only testify to it. The truth claims of Christianity are not easily validated externally. They are a matter of faith."[87]

Second, Peter offered a direct appeal in response to their conviction. His response offers a straightforward path to salvation through repentance and baptism. However, a controversy exists within Peter's pairing of repentance and baptism. Is Peter contending for baptism as a condition of forgiveness of sins? Polhill offered clarity when he asserted, "[The word] *eis* can also mean 'on the ground of, on the basis of,' which would indicate the opposite relationship—that the forgiveness of sins is the basis, the grounds

83. Bock, *Acts*, 136.

84. Bruce, *Book of the Acts*, 68.

85. Osborne, *Acts*, 56.

86. Bock, *Acts*, 141.

87. William Willimon, "Assuming They Are Christians," in Brown et al., *Voice in the Wilderness*, 66.

for being baptized."[88] To this extent, the New Testament use of *eis* in Acts 2:38 connects the saving reign of Christ with the fulfillment of salvation expressed through human response.[89] Essentially, obedience demonstrated through baptism is predicated upon belief demonstrated through repentance. Although Bock disagreed with Polhill's understanding of *eis*, he conceded that Polhill was correct: "Repentance is the key response."[90]

Finally, in response to repentance and baptism, Peter contends for the promise of the Holy Spirit. He has now come full circle to what initiated the speech in the first place—the infilling of the Holy Spirit (v. 4). What is more, Peter offers the assurance of salvation, *sothete*, offered through Jesus. Peter anchors his confidence in the conclusion of his argument and returns to the prophet Joel. Osborne asserted, "They will rescue themselves by repenting and believing. It is God who justifies sinners. It is better to translate the passive command with permissive force, 'Let yourselves be saved.'"[91]

## Conclusion

Peter's sermon set out to convince his Jewish audience of Jesus' messiahship and the fulfillment of Old Testament prophecies. By linking Jesus' resurrection and exaltation to the outpouring of the Holy Spirit, Peter calls his listeners to recognize Jesus as the promised Messiah and respond to the gospel message. John Stott asserted, "At Pentecost, the prophetic witness of the Old Testament was added to by Peter's testimony as apostle. He proclaimed Jesus as Messiah and Lord, the Holy Spirit confirmed his words with power, and the believing people of God became the Spirit-filled Body of Christ. God himself performed this creative work by his Spirit through his Word."[92] Peter's kerygma exemplifies the early Christian practice of interpreting the Old Testament, considering the events of Jesus' life, death, and resurrection. It serves as a foundational text for the doctrine of Jesus' resurrection and the role of the Holy Spirit in the life of the church. Ultimately, Peter's kerygma gives light to the ubiquity of Christ in the Old Testament and offers an example of preaching the gospel grounded in Scripture.

88. Polhill, *Acts*, 117.

89. See Albrecht Oepke, "εἰς," in Kittel et al., *Theological Dictionary of the New Testament*, 429.

90. Bock, *Acts*, 144.

91. Osborne, *Acts*, 59–60.

92. Stott, *God's Word*, 39.

Peter's sermon emphasizes the fulfillment of Old Testament prophecy, the reality of Jesus' resurrection, and the outpouring of the Holy Spirit.

What is more, Peter's kerygma functions as a powerful testament to Jesus' messianic role and the transformative impact of the Holy Spirit. The transformation of the gospel extends beyond mere knowledge of the head. Also, it does not merely consist of an emotional mountaintop experience. Ultimately, Peter's call to his audience acknowledges the necessity of the rhetorical persuasion of the whole person through the emotions (their hearts pierced, or the *pathos*), the mind (Old Testament appeal of the gospel, or the *logos*), and the volition (the call to obedience to Christ as Peter had, or the *ethos*). The response to this divine revelation attests to the complexity of the summons of the text. This expectation to respond to Christ is explicit—the call to the emotions, to the mind, and to obedience, both to justification and to sanctification.

# CHAPTER 5

# The Gospel Demands a Preacher

As we have seen, the message of Jesus Christ is woven into the very fabric of Scripture such that the gospel connection exists within each pericope. The hope of the gospel message resides in the expression of the glory of God through Christ in the working out of redemption and salvation. Faithful exposition demands seeing the text through the eyes of proper exegesis. The gospel is central to the revelation of Scripture. This message centers on the central themes Paul describes in 1 Cor 15. The message of the gospel (though some contest its implications) revolves centrally around the person and work of Jesus Christ.

Regarding the New Testament message of the gospel, Greg Gilbert wrote, "First the bad news: God is your judge, and you have sinned against him. And then the gospel: but Jesus has died so that sinners may be forgiven of their sins if they will repent and believe in him."[1] The consistency of the person and work of Jesus in the New Testament kerygma message cannot be overstated. This chapter will examine Rom 10:4–17 and show how Paul argues that the proclamation of the gospel demands a preacher. The crux of Paul's argument rests in verses 13–14. He wrote,

> For "Whoever will call on the name of the Lord will be saved." How then will they call on Him in whom they have not believed? How will they believe in Him whom they have not heard? And how will they hear without a preacher? How will they preach unless they are sent? Just as it is written, "How beautiful are the feet of those who bring good news of good things." (Rom 10:13–14)

1. Gilbert, *What Is the Gospel?*, 36.

Paul's gospel focus was foundational in the message he preached. Moreover, Paul demonstrated a preaching theology within Rom 10 that established a golden chain of preaching. He established the connection between the centrality of Christ, the preacher's call to preach, the message they proclaim, the hearer's response through confession and belief, and the result of the gospel through dependence upon Christ. This salvation leads to, and ultimately culminates in, the glory of God in Christ. Ultimately, preachers can apply Paul's methodology contextually and universally. The extent of Paul's influence through the gospel message aims to exalt the risen Christ Jesus. The substance and content of Paul's kerygma consistently focused on the person and work of Jesus Christ.[2]

As every sermon should exalt Christ, so every sermon should sanctify and save. Just as the text confronts us with more than mere words, it delivers a summons—a call, a compelling charge, a demand that must not be ignored, urging us to respond. Every sermon must elucidate both the salvific and sanctifying work of the cross over the lives of the congregation. Adam Hughes articulated, "Not only can a pastor be committed to expository and evangelistic preaching simultaneously, but it is a must and biblically consistent with doing so."[3] This conviction rests upon the truth that the single greatest need for the lost is the saving work of the gospel of Jesus. Conversely, the single greatest need of the believer is the sanctifying work of the gospel of Jesus. C. Kyle Walker attested, "Felt needs are often genuine needs. Nevertheless, they are not always the deepest needs. Text-driven preaching trusts that God knows man's needs and allows Scripture, rather than man's needs, to set the homiletical agenda."[4] Expositional preaching is the most effective way to draw on the work of the cross. However, every preaching of Scripture demands the gospel, and that preaching demands a preacher.

## The Preacher's Call to Proclamation

First, let us establish the occasion for the writing of the letter to the Romans. This occasion sets the tone for Paul's intention. The context allows the reader to understand Paul's mind while penning the words within the letter of Romans. It is likely that Paul—although aware of the circumstances

2. Griffiths, *Preaching in the New Testament*, 33.

3. Adam Hughes, "The Soul of the Evangelistic Expository Sermon," in Price, *Engage*, 446.

4. Walker, *Let the Text Talk*, 109.

surrounding the church in Rome—wrote intentionally, irrespective of temporal issues, and honed in on the eternal implications of the gospel of Jesus Christ.[5] Paul demonstrated his theological position regardless of his view of the culture by addressing Jewish-gentile relational dynamics. He asserted, "To the Jew first and also to the Greek" (1:16b). Vital to understanding the context of the letter to the Romans is recognizing Paul's abiding dependence on the Old Testament in presenting his doctrines.[6] He introduced his audience to the concept of the ubiquity of Christ as foretold by Old Testament prophets. In his address, he declared that he was "set apart for the gospel of God, which He promised beforehand through His prophets in the holy Scriptures" (1:1b–2). Robert Plummer asserted, "For Paul, his divine commission to bring the salvation of God to a fallen world was nothing other than his defense and proclamation of the gospel."[7] Paul's declaration of the necessity of the preacher establishes his conviction that his calling was to the proclamation of the gospel. The kerygma served as a foundational component of Paul's missionary method. Paul's encounter with Jesus on the road to Damascus (see Acts 9) shifted his passion from religious zeal and persecution to an all-consuming love for Jesus and his church.

## The Message We Proclaim

In Rom 10:4–8, Paul addresses the righteousness of the law and the righteousness of faith. He spent verses 1–3 declaring his desire for Israel's salvation, but noting that their righteousness was self-established and not of the knowledge of God's righteousness. He concludes his argument by drawing on the image of Christ woven into the Old Testament. Rather than imposing Christ as another God among gods, Paul demonstrates a commitment to God's redemption of believers through the revelation of Christ within Deut 30. We can see four key aspects within this section: (1) the law versus faith; (2) Christ as fulfillment; (3) the accessibility of salvation; and (4) the continuity with Moses.

5. Dunn, *Romans 1–8*, xlv.

6. Carson and Moo, *Introduction to the New Testament*, 373.

7. Plummer, *Paul's Understanding*, 45.

## *The Law and the Gospel*

Beginning in verses 4 and 5, Paul builds his argument for the two ways of seeking salvation: the way of the law and the way of faith. He illustrated both positions from Old Testament passages, establishing an encapsulation of the law. The term *righteousness* in this context means "right with God," and the phrase "based on law" is understood in light of righteousness arising from obedience to the law.[8] Paul referenced Lev 18:5. In his theological reflection, Paul demonstrated that every Jew would have understood that obedience to the law means blessings from the Lord, and the converse is also true. Moo noted that the life in view here—as typically seen in the Pentateuch—is the blessing of God's covenantal promises: health, fruitful crops, and security in the land.[9]

Paul also reveals that righteousness came in two ways: obedience to the law and faith in Christ. In addressing righteousness by adherence to the law, he presented the negative of the righteousness of faith in Christ. Moo asserted, "Paul stated this principle as a warning to Jews who refuse to submit to the righteousness of God in Christ."[10] Further, Paul compelled his hearers to understand that his view of justification by faith was rooted in Scripture. Leon Morris noted that the importance of Paul's argument was not "some new-fangled idea" but God's demonstration of always accepting people based on faith.[11] Finally, Paul's use of the word *for* builds the connection between the law and faith. Moo states, "[*For*] introduces all of vv. 5–8 as an elaboration of the connection between righteousness and faith and its significance."[12]

Paul uses Lev 18:5 to distill the essence of the law. According to the context of Lev 18:5, the primary effect of the law was to lead to life. Essentially, life would result if a person could perform all of the law's requirements.[13] Mark Rooker noted that four truths exist when reading Lev 18:1–5 in conjunction with Deut 30:1–20. He observed,

> (1) Depraved human beings are justified only by the grace of regeneration; (2) justification is always by faith; (3) God has always

8. Newman and Nida, *Paul's Letter to the Romans*, 198.
9. Moo, *Letter to the Romans*, 664.
10. Moo, *Letter to the Romans*, 664.
11. Morris, *Epistle to the Romans*, 381.
12. Moo, *Letter to the Romans*, 665.
13. Mounce, *Romans*, 208.

> demanded that his children love him wholeheartedly; and (4) the Law of God is always internalized by the people of faith. The phrase "the man who obeys them will live by them" should thus be viewed as promising a meaningful, secure life for those who are faithful to God and who exhibit their faithfulness by obedience to the Law. Hence, the verse pertains more to sanctification than justification.[14]

The outward demonstration would result from internalizing the law of God in the hearts of its hearers. René Péter-Contesse and John Ellington asserted that the root of abundant life is obedience to God's commands as recorded throughout the Bible.[15] Nevertheless, John Calvin identified the crux of man's obedience. He asserted,

> For, although God might in His own right require what He pleased, such is His kindness to men that He chose to entice them by promises to obey Him freely. Since the hope of reward naturally attracts us, we are slow and lazy until some fruit appears. Consequently, God voluntarily promises to arouse them from their sloth, that if men obey His Law, He will repay them.[16]

Man's propensity toward laziness concerning the law reinforces Paul's connection to Christ. Paul illuminated the truth that Christ alone fulfilled the demands of the law by his sinless life and sacrificial death. Colin Kruse asserted, "Paul is implying that Christ is the 'end' of the law (he brings its era to a close) and its 'goal' (he is what the law anticipated and pointed toward)."[17]

With this understanding, Paul used Leviticus to capture how Christ was the end of the law of righteousness for those who believe. He argued that the fulfillment of the law is found only in Christ. But the law, in and of itself, is bound to works because its existence demands obedience.[18] Paul's use of Lev 18:5 is succinct and summarizes the essence of the law: blessings resulting from obedience. Only the one who obeys the law perfectly may find life through it.[19]

14. Rooker, *Leviticus*, 240–41.
15. Péter-Contesse and Ellington, *Handbook on Leviticus*, 271.
16. Calvin, *Four Last Books of Moses*, 202 (on Lev 18).
17. Kruse, *Paul's Letter to the Romans*, 405.
18. Barrett, *Epistle to the Romans*, 185.
19. Moo, *Letter to the Romans*, 666.

Paul presented the gospel by demonstrating that Christ fulfilled the law. The standard of obedience was repeatedly, systematically rejected—save by Christ. Throughout history, humanity has failed to achieve the perfect standard of the law. Therefore, Paul's argument begins with building the connection between righteousness and faith by considering the law.

### *The Centrality of Christ*

In Rom 10:6–7, Paul presented a counterargument to his encapsulation of the law. He then connected the Old Testament Scriptures to Christ, revealing the Christocentric connection to those passages. In accomplishing this, Paul showed the connection. J. P. Lange and F. R. Fay wrote, "There are here two antitheses: first, that of the externality of the law and the inwardness of the gospel; second, that of doing and experiencing."[20] To the first, Paul's use of "Do not say in your heart" drew on Deut 9:4. This phrasing further solidified his claim of justification by faith, as the essence of his argument rested on God having done all that is necessary.[21] For the second, Paul used Deuteronomy to show that the righteousness of faith is rooted in and flows through the righteousness of the law—the person and work of Christ.

The crux of the issue is that no one can perfectly meet the requirements of the law. The law ultimately points to Christ, but itself holds no power to supply salvation. Instead, it points in the right direction and was never intended for man to earn God's favor.[22] The law pointed in the right direction, but Christ provided the means to fulfill the law. Calvin asserted that Paul's connection was valid: "Wherefore Paul most truly concludes that this is the word of faith preached in the Gospel; both because the Law does not efficaciously lead men to God, and because the keeping of it is impossible, on account of its extreme rigor."[23]

Next, Paul utilizes a fragment of Deut 30:12–13: "Who will go up to heaven for us?" and "Who will cross the sea for us?" These seemingly out-of-place assertions create the essence of the task's impossibility. Instead, Paul builds the argument that the uniqueness of Christ's work was only achievable by him. Moo identified "descending to the abyss" and "ascending

20. Lange and Fay, *Paul to the Romans*, 343.

21. Morris, *Epistle to the Romans*, 382.

22. Mounce, *Romans*, 207.

23. Calvin, *Four Last Books of Moses*, 414 (on Deut 29).

to heaven" as proverbial terms for the impossible task of human beings.[24] Robert Mounce elaborated, "It is the reality of this resurrection that lends credence to all that Jesus did and taught throughout his earthly life. It is God's way of authenticating to us that Jesus is the Son of God."[25]

### *Salvation Is Accessible*

Verse 8 establishes the Old Testament's theological underpinning for the declaration of the gospel message of Christ. In verse 8, Paul leveraged Deut 30:14 to connect the gospel's message with the nearness of God. He then provided his proposition for preaching the gospel—salvation and righteousness through confession and faith. Charles Simeon asserted, "We are told, in few words, what was 'the word of faith which Paul preached.' Two things he insisted on, as indispensably necessary to our salvation—faith in Christ as our crucified and risen Savior and a public confession of him under that character."[26] There exists both conditions—confession and belief—and we would do well to pay attention to their ordering. The confession and belief connection of Paul is revealed in his "word of faith" to the description of the word in Deut 30:14 as being "in your mouth" and "in your heart."[27] His connection to the Old Testament established the fidelity of the message delivered to the prophets and fulfilled in Christ. Therefore, the message of faith is not a fanciful narrative but a culmination of the divine plan proclaimed in the Old Testament.

Paul connected his thoughts to Deut 30:14 to continue the defense of his "word of faith." The verb for "we are preaching" is in the present tense and indicates Paul's current activity. Paul alluded to the Old Testament to reinforce the weight of his proclaimed gospel message. Morris identified this as "denoting the habitual act."[28] Paul defended the "word of faith" (*rhema*) that he was preaching as grounded in both Scripture and his obedience. Paul believed that salvation is resultant from faith alone and that God himself provides it.[29] In agreement with this, Mounce articulated that genuine faith is available for anyone who believes and confesses that Jesus is

24. Moo, *Letter to the Romans*, 672.
25. Mounce, *Romans*, 210.
26. Simeon, *Romans*, 386.
27. Moo, *Letter to the Romans*, 675.
28. Morris, *Epistle to the Romans*, 384.
29. Barrett, *Epistle to the Romans*, 185.

Lord.[30] The Messiah had already appeared, and his act of divine redemption had been carried out. The distinction lies in the fact that this redemptive act was not a reward for legal righteousness but an act of God's grace.[31] Further, the issue was not in keeping the word of the Lord but rather knowing the word.[32] Essentially, the word of faith points to the message of Christ, culminating in Christ as the heavenly Lord, crucified and risen.

### *The Continuity with Moses*

Paul shows that the Old Testament anticipated righteousness by faith, not just by works. He demonstrated that to proclaim "the word of faith which we are preaching" is to declare the path of salvation to the lost. He shows that the same "word" that is near in Deuteronomy connects directly to the gospel message. James Stuart put it best when he wrote,

> There is ultimately only one problem of communication of the Christian message—the problem of allowing myself, yourself, as the messengers, to be taken command of by the risen Christ. For the crux of evangelism still lies in that one dramatic paradox, which some scholars disparage and discount as unpractical mysticism and apostolic rhetoric, but which in point of fact is vibrant with the most practical and decisive force in all the world: "I, yet not I, but Christ."[33]

The message Paul proclaimed was the death, burial, and resurrection of Christ. The central focus of Paul's task was singularly on the preaching of the gospel as his primary goal. The content of Paul's kerygma, time and again, was Christ's death, burial, and resurrection with the expectation of a response.

## Response Through Belief and Confession

Verses 9 and 10 clearly set forth Paul's expectation—both a belief and its expression through confession. The use of *Lord* connotes the position held

30. Mounce, *Romans*, 208.
31. Barrett, *Epistle to the Romans*, 186.
32. Merrill, *Deuteronomy*, 391.
33. Stuart, *A Faith to Proclaim*, 47.

by Christ, while the word *raised* establishes the action done. Ultimately, these verses demonstrate a chiastic structure of A-B-B-A.

$A_1$: confessing with your mouth

$B_1$: believing in your heart

$B_2$: believing results in righteousness

$A_2$: confessing results in salvation

The confession of Christ's lordship demonstrates fealty to his authority, while the belief in the truthfulness of his resurrection demonstrates submission to his power. The lordship of Christ was fundamental to Paul's preaching, and that submission is the necessary response from the hearer.[34] Therefore, Paul anchored his preaching on the authority of Christ's lordship and the power of his resurrection.

The statement "Jesus is Lord" is one of the oldest confessions of Christian belief (Matt 16:13–20, Mark 8:27–30, Luke 9:18–21). Paul's audience understood this term. He expounded his argument by elaborating on the need to "believe" that it was God who "raised" Christ from the dead. This distinction arose to establish the uniqueness of the claim of Christianity—Christ's resurrection. Paul attested in his letter to the church at Corinth: "If Christ has not been raised, then our preaching is in vain, your faith also is in vain" (1 Cor 15:14). Paul connected the "nearness of the word of faith" to the act of confessing Christ. Therefore, the kerygma implies a positive response through faith and a declaration of what Christ has done.[35] The proclamation of the gospel, *euangelion*, further expects a response from its hearers. A clear understanding of the implications of the kerygma is essential in seeing the gospel message proclaimed to humanity through his chosen means—the testimony of his witnesses.[36] Paul demonstrated this by showing the simplicity of the message and its required response as twofold: "confess with your mouth" and "believe in your heart" (Rom 10:9). Ultimately, true faith in Christ must encompass confession and belief, and the fact that they are not distinct activities but rather two sides of the same coin as expressions of faith in Jesus.[37]

34. Kruse, *Paul's Letter to the Romans*, 409–10.

35. Drummond, *Word of the Cross*, 204.

36. Queen, "Theological Assessment," 40.

37. Kruse, *Paul's Letter to the Romans*, 410.

The gospel message preached by Paul and, one could argue, by the rest of the apostles provided a clear call for fealty to and belief in Christ. The apostles rooted their kerygma—what Paul calls the word of faith—in the confession of Christ as Lord and in the belief in the resurrection. Therein lies an expectation of both the right belief and the right response. The exaltation of Jesus as Lord was a distinct and central component of the Christian confession, encompassing the belief that God raised Jesus from the dead.[38] The intrinsic connection lies in the fact that confession is an outward expression of a deep-seated conviction from within a person's inner recesses.[39] Faith in Christ must stem from an inward conviction of the fundamental truth of the resurrection. Paul asserted, "And if Christ has not been raised, your faith is worthless; you are still in your sins" (1 Cor 15:17). The resurrection is the central component of the Christian faith. The "word of faith" Paul proclaimed is the good news of Jesus Christ, wrapped up in his death, burial, and subsequent resurrection.

Paul's response was that confession and belief in the authority and power of Christ result in salvation. Preaching repentance (confession) and belief in Christ are essential components of Paul's kerygma. Zane Pratt elucidated, "The redeeming work of Christ is appropriated by sinful men and women only through repentance from sin and faith in Jesus Christ, which are themselves gifts of God through the work of the Holy Spirit."[40]

## Result of the Gospel

Upon the foundation of the gospel, Paul established his conviction of the necessity of kerygma. Verses 11–13 continue by elucidating the reward of the good news proclaimed. The effectual result of confession and belief culminates in righteousness and salvation. Belief in Christ does not disappoint. In Christ, there is no shame or disgrace and no distinction between "Jew and Greek" (Rom 10:12). There exists a connection in Paul's declaration with Rom 3:23; "he who believes" is supported by the emphasis that "all have sinned and fall short of the glory of God" and that the divine act of grace justifies both freely.[41] Therefore, all, without distinction of being

38. Moo, *Letter to the Romans*, 675.

39. Mounce, *Romans*, 209.

40. Zane Pratt, "The Heart of Mission: Redemption," in Ashford, *Theology and Practice*, 58.

41. Kruse, *Paul's Letter to the Romans*, 410.

Jew or gentile, have sinned against God and have fallen short of his Holy standard.[42]

The culmination of Paul's attestation that "the same Lord is Lord of all" implicitly points back to the declaration of confession of Christ as Lord (Rom 10:9, 12). The Lord declared here is Jesus, and, as such, his positional authority demands fealty from all, irrespective of their Jew or gentile position before God.[43] The result of that allegiance is the outpouring of riches from God—salvation. The biblical understanding of *soteria* holds that, as used by biblical writers, salvation conveys either deliverance from physical dangers or the spiritual security of the eternal soul. In either instance, the concept of deliverance is a prominent theme in salvation and is the reward tethered to the gospel for those who "call on" Christ. It is essential to note that Paul's use of "call on," when coupled with the personal object, signifies looking outside oneself for assistance. The "call on" here is appealing to the lordship and power of Christ from the previously established "confession" and "belief." The "call on" is connected to confession and belief in response to preaching, resulting in salvation. Charles Simeon stated, "All the blessings of salvation, if only you believe in Christ, are yours: yours is that peace of God which passeth all understanding: yours are all the treasures both of grace and glory; holiness is yours, as well as pardon; for the faith that brings you into a state of peace with God will 'work by love,' and 'purify the heart.'"[44]

Paul's motivation rested upon his indebtedness to Christ and his being Christ's ambassador to the nations. Michael Green asserted, "It was through the preaching of the gospel by humble folk who do not advertise themselves but confidently proclaim the lordship of Jesus that God's light breaks into blinded hearts."[45] In Paul's estimation, this gospel was then the "power of God for salvation," the outworking of his obligation (Rom 1:13–16). Moreover, Paul asserted, "Whoever will call on the name of the Lord will be saved" (Joel 2:32, Rom 10:13). The New Testament usage of *euangelion* was the verbal proclamation, and the New Testament does not refer to a written document or literary genre but rather a "good news" message of hope and forgiveness that brings joy to the hearer.[46]

42. Barrett, *Epistle to the Romans*, 188.

43. Moo, *Letter to the Romans*, 678.

44. Simeon, *Romans*, 394.

45. Green, *Evangelism in the Early Church*, 292.

46. Queen, "Theological Assessment," 40.

## The Connection Between Proclamation and Belief

Paul entered this section with a series of questions, each building from the next in a seemingly systematic reversal of order. Paul suggested that one cannot "call on" apart from a firm grasp of "confession" and "belief" in Christ. If salvation is "calling on" the Lord, Paul built the connection to the kerygma. Robert Mounce asserted, "The essence of Paul's argument is seen if we put his six verbs in the opposite order: Christ sends heralds; heralds preach; people hear; hearers believe; believers call; and those who call are saved."[47] Implicit in this ordering is the saving relationship with Christ that results. With that in mind, we can see Christ bookended. Christ commissions the messenger, and it is Christ who receives the hearer into his church. We could even infer the role of those who believe in completing the cycle and evangelizing the lost.[48] With this ordering, Paul built a bridge from salvation back to the proclamation of the gospel message and to the call of those preachers by Christ toward the kerygma. I see this as a golden chain of preaching that connects the gospel message completely to Christ. As Paul wrote, "For from Him and through Him and to Him are all things. To Him be the glory forever. Amen" (Rom 11:36). The power of the gospel proclamation rests in the lordship and power of Christ and not the musings of the orator.[49] The power of the gospel rests upon the one who sends the message and the one whom the message is about—Jesus Christ.

Paul's depiction of the gospel process drew specific attention to the messenger. He quoted the prophet Isaiah:

> How lovely on the mountains
> Are the feet of him who brings good news,
> Who announces peace
> And brings good news of happiness,
> Who announces salvation,
> And says to Zion, "Your God reigns."
> (Isa 52:7)

Paul's depiction of a messenger connected to the New Testament period's understanding of *euangelion*. In Greek literature outside the New Testament, the *euangelion* generally refers to news of victory, often related

47. Mounce, *Romans*, 211.

48. Osborne, *Romans*, 321.

49. Morris, *Epistle to the Romans*, 390.

to a battle.[50] Eckhard Schnabel observed that Paul connected his preaching of the gospel to the "messengers in ancient Greece sent from the battlefield to the army's home city, which awaited the news of the victory of the army."[51] Paul was leveraging the victory declaration within the "good news" of Isaiah to capture the *soterian* language. Paul recognized that the gospel "is the power of God for salvation" (Rom 1:16). The messenger of the good news of the gospel is declaring the ultimate and eternal victory of Christ. Scripture does not neglect the parallels but instead attaches to their salvific intent toward a declaration of victory.

Paul uses the metaphor of feet to describe the beauty of the messenger. The reference to feet strikes a deep cultural tone. Feet were the primary means of travel and were extremely filthy from the road, covered in dirt and sweat. Historically, we know that the primary mode of transportation was walking, and as such, feet would be dirty and smelly after a long, hot journey. However, to those who eagerly awaited the good news they carried, they were beautiful, and those who brought good news were always welcome.[52] Paul Washer beautifully described this when he wrote,

> Take note of the words *beautiful* or *lovely*. The gospel is such good news to the discerning and believing heart that it is said to "beautify" or "make lovely" even the calloused and soiled feet of the messenger who brings it! Imagine the fear and hopelessness of a condemned prisoner only moments before his execution. But as the hangman tightens the noose, a messenger runs up the stairs of the gallows, crying out, "Good news! Good news! The king has granted pardon!" Although the messenger is soaked in sweat and the mire of the street, he is beautified by his message and the prisoner embraces him without reservation.[53]

Moreover, the temporal news of victory brought such joy; yet, how much more the eternal declaration of victory would bring lasting joy. Essentially, the "feet" of those who proclaim the gospel of Christ bring hope and joy due to the lasting nature of the message.

50. Queen, "Theological Assessment," 38.
51. Schnabel, *Paul the Missionary*, 210.
52. Morris, *Epistle to the Romans*, 391.
53. Washer, *Preeminent Christ*, 15.

## The Hearing of the Word of Christ

Paul built an argument that drove the significance of the kerygma within the process of salvation. In verse 16, Paul drew upon a peculiar distinction that seemingly breaks the chain of salvation from the call to repentance. Israel had rejected the prophetic and the apostolic witness to Christ and was ultimately responsible for this rejection.[54] Moreover, Paul continued that faith comes from hearing the word of Christ. He ultimately contended that "belief" in Christ directly results from the "proclamation" of Christ. In verse 17, Paul established that the spoken word produces faith, enabling sinners to call upon Christ. Kruse succinctly summed up the section: "Faith, then, is generated through the preaching of the gospel (through the ministry of the Holy Spirit)."[55]

One cannot overstate the necessity of the kerygma established by Paul. Fundamentally, the kerygma serves as God's method of salvation. Therefore, the kerygma results in the miraculous—the conversion of rebellious sinners to fealty to Christ.[56] Paul's conviction is summed up best by Charles Simeon: "If preachers will unite in extending the knowledge of the gospel, thousands shall in due time arise to attest and to rejoice in the tidings we proclaim. Yes, 'the Gospel of peace' will be received by them as 'glad tidings of good things.'"[57] The Pauline kerygma serves the end of evangelization, fosters faith, and connects diverse communities to the central message of salvation through Christ. Paul did not have a deliberate methodology or plan for proclaiming the gospel, yet he was still guided by definitive principles anchored in the very gospel itself.[58] These principles derive from an understanding of the Pauline kerygma.

## Conclusion

The exegetical analysis of Rom 10:8–17 elucidated Paul's kerygmatic focus as foundational to his mission. Paul demonstrated that at the core of his method in Rom 10 is the sending of a preacher. His preaching theology established a golden chain of preaching and, by proxy, his evangelistic

54. Barrett, *Epistle to the Romans*, 190.

55. Kruse, *Paul's Letter to the Romans*, 418.

56. Drummond, *Word of the Cross*, 204.

57. Simeon, *Romans*, 393.

58. Allen, *Missionary Methods*, 14.

methodology. Paul revealed the connection between the preacher's call, the message they proclaim, the hearer's response through confession and belief, the response of dependence upon Christ, and the salvation that ensues. Ultimately, Christ commissions those who preach, and it is Christ who receives the lost into his kingdom. The extent of Paul's influence through the gospel message aims to exalt the risen Christ Jesus. The substance and content of Paul's kerygma consistently focused on the person and work of Jesus Christ.[59] This theology of preaching shows us the necessity of a preacher. It also shows that man's greatest need is the saving gospel of Christ.

The Pauline kerygma serves the end of evangelization, fosters faith, and connects diverse communities to the central message of salvation through Christ. These principles derive from an understanding of Paul's theology of preaching outlined in Rom 10. J. Josh Smith argued, "If God has spoken, and he has spoken for a purpose, the responsibility of the preacher is to not only preach His Word (2 Tim 4:2) but also to preach so that people might respond to His Word."[60] The expectation of obedience in response to the gospel is explicit—the summons of the text toward salvation to all who believe and confess.

Additionally, Paul's appeal to the golden chain of preaching demonstrates the necessity of the rhetorical persuasion of the whole person through the mind (they hear the gospel, or the *logos*), the emotions (with the heart they believe, or the *pathos*), and the volition (the confession of Christ, or the *ethos*). Paul expressed the chain of events that necessitate the response to the gospel within the complexity of the summons of the text, as established through his use of the Old Testament. This expectation to respond to Christ is explicit—the call to the mind, to the emotions, and to volition through obedience. This call of the summons of the text is fully displayed in a call to salvation—a call to be justified before God and a call to sanctification through him. This call to respond to the text stands as the greatest need of the church—the proclamation of the gospel of Jesus Christ.

The next chapter will address the greatest needs of the church. Before we delve into that topic as it relates to the summons, I wanted to share one of my favorite quotes on preaching. What motivates our preaching? Steven Smith wrote, "If immediate emotional response is the primary goal of preaching, then it logically misses the significant point of preaching:

59. Griffiths, *Preaching in the New Testament*, 33.

60. Smith, *Preaching for a Verdict*, 31.

long-term results."[61] I share this because it is beyond my control whether the audience responds favorably to the sermon. We all like the accolades of a well-delivered sermon.

Nevertheless, a sermon that depends upon my eloquence and rigorous study falls short of the mark time and again. Instead, let us strive toward the one thing we can control: faithfulness to the text. Let us seek, as our end, to re-present the text with the same Holy Spirit–laden power as the original authors. The greatest need of the church is not my fanciful speech but the power of the Holy Spirit brought to bear in the faithful preaching of the word of God.

61. Smith, *Dying to Preach*, 117.

# CHAPTER 6

# The Greatest Need of the Church

THE GREATEST NEED IN the church today is to preach Christ. Paul clarified this point in his charge to "preach the word" in 2 Tim 4. Paul demonstrated an obligation to proclaim the complete gospel of the goodness of redemption for those who believe and the wrath of God against those who reject Christ. Paul's charge to Timothy to fulfill his ministry identifies imperatives of pastoral ministry that encapsulate the commands of preaching and the spiritual discipline of evangelism. Luke demonstrated the ubiquity of Christ throughout all of Scripture, showing that the pericope of the text reveals the gospel. The previous chapter unpacked the necessity of the preacher to proclaim the gospel from the pulpit. This chapter seeks as its aim to establish that the greatest need of the church is gospel preaching that exalts Christ and exhorts the congregation to respond. Greater than felt-needs preaching is preaching submitted to the transformative power of the declaration of the risen Christ. Steven Smith stated, "Surrendered communication is the relinquishing of our right to say anything we want any way we want. It is limiting our own freedom of expression in order to maximize effectiveness and minimize self-interest."[1] This is, in my estimation, the greatest need of the church—fewer preachers filling the air with their opinions and diatribes; more men of God surrendered to the charge of Paul to Timothy to "preach the word" (2 Tim 4:2).

This chapter will examine the call to preach the word in Paul's charge to Timothy in 2 Tim 4:1–5. Two things will become apparent in its examination. First, this is a letter; therefore, Paul's writing is propositional. An analysis of the independent clauses "preach the word" and "do the work of

1. Smith, *Dying to Preach*, 115.

an evangelist" (vv. 2, 5) comes immediately to the forefront of Paul's argumentation. Additionally, they serve as imperatives that hold expectations of the hearer's response. The structure of Paul's writing here seems to be in three sections: the charge of Timothy for treatment of the word of the gospel; the reason for the charge to preach the word; and finally, the internal charge to Timothy to guard his character in light of the gospel message he proclaims.

Second, the historical setting of Paul's writing illuminates his imprisonment. Couple that knowledge with the solemn charge and his expectation of death in verse 6, and the preacher concludes the somber occasion of its writing. Paul is essentially passing the baton to his ministry partner, Timothy. No matter how grave the circumstance, the tone also provides hopeful undertones—Paul is ready to be with Jesus. He wrote, "I have fought the good fight, I have finished the course, I have kept the faith" (2 Tim 4:7). This examination of the spirit of the text provides a greater understanding of the feeling. Paul looked back without regret or remorse.

The occasion of Paul's writing was the direst of circumstances. Paul was in prison (2 Tim 1:8) and completed his first court hearing (4:16–18). Lonely and abandoned by Demas, Paul sat in prison expectantly awaiting his death (4:6–8, 10). Nevertheless, ever resolute in his passion and commitment to the gospel, he exhorted Timothy to be faithful to the gospel in Timothy's ministry. Although authorship has come into question in modern scholarship, the validity of the authorship, in part, rests upon the historical acceptance of the Pastoral Epistles for nearly fifteen hundred years, and it argues that dissent from Pauline authorship rests on a shaky foundation and ultimately poses major doctrinal issues.[2]

In 2 Tim 4:1–5, Paul admonished Timothy toward pastoral ministry. Paul's charge to Timothy is to "preach the word" (v. 2). The language of the remainder of the aorist imperatives flows from this first. We would do well to acknowledge Steven Smith's caution when he wrote, "We are tempted to reference Paul's admonition to preach the word (2 Tim 4:2). However, while Paul's admonition to Timothy is clear enough, it is more an admonition to faithfulness explaining Christ from all of Scripture than it is advocating a philosophy of preaching."[3] Understanding that the charge is to faithful proclamation of the message of Christ is clear in Paul's instruction

2. See Andreas J. Köstenberger, "Hermeneutical and Exegetical Challenges in Interpreting the *Pastoral Epistles*," in Köstenberger and Wilder, *Entrusted with the Gospel*, 2–3.

3. Smith, *Recapturing the Voice of God*, 22.

culminating in "fulfill your ministry" (v. 5). In particular, the aorist imperatives woven throughout this section indicate that the actions are the result of something that has happened in the past. This past action now gives rise to the actions that Paul commands the preacher to take in the present. The actions Paul commands of Timothy directly result from the work already carried out on the cross. In the context of the passage, the responsibility of Timothy toward the proclamation of the gospel through preaching and the work of evangelism is interrelated with the same end. Paul further illustrated the significance of this connection by referencing Timothy's gospel work to other churches (Phil 2:22, 1 Thess 3:2).[4] Therefore, the charge wraps up the urgency of Paul's imminent departure. Paul's charge to Timothy to fulfill his ministry identifies imperatives of pastoral ministry that encapsulate the commands of both preaching and the work of evangelism.

## The Weight of the Charge

In 2 Tim 4:1, Paul reinforced his command to Timothy with two oaths. Paul emphasized the nature of the oaths in his use of the phrase "I solemnly charge." There exists a grammatical awkwardness in Paul's use of the prepositional phrase *in the presence of*.[5] Paul's use of the phrase is to remind Timothy of his responsibility.[6] Thus, Paul likely used *in the presence of* as a literary method to command his readers' attention. He is drawing out the solemn charge's importance in preaching the word of God, particularly considering God and Christ's second coming. The *and* serves to compound the charge by joining God and Jesus and then adding the coming of Christ.[7] Even so, the traditional kingdom language, as seen in "His appearing and His kingdom," is rare in the Pastoral Epistles and appears only here in the final chapter (vv. 1, 18).[8] This language reinforces the severity and urgency of the claim. Against the backdrop of these absolutes, Paul built his charge to Timothy.

4. Knight, *Pastoral Epistles*, 450.
5. Mounce, *Pastoral Epistles*, 571.
6. Knight, *Pastoral Epistles*, 452.
7. Heckert, *Discourse Function of Conjoiners*, 106.
8. Collins, *1 & 2 Timothy*, 268.

## Preach the Word

In 2 Tim 4:2, Paul provided five aorist imperatives. These commands indicate urgency regardless of their frequency or duration. The implication of the present aorist imperatives is "make it your habit to do" and "do whenever the situation arises."[9] Paul's charge to "preach the word" does not indicate how often or for how long. There is no prescribed cadence to which Timothy is bound. Furthermore, there is no end to his obedience. Therefore, Timothy is to preach the word as often as possible and as long as he holds breath in his lungs.

Additionally, each of the other imperatives builds upon the first imperative: "preach the word." These imperatives loosely parallel the points identified previously in Paul's declaration of Scripture's purpose—teaching, reproof, correction, and training in righteousness (2 Tim 3:16). Paul's command to Timothy is to preach the gospel message of the person and work of Christ.[10] It is worth noting that the anaphoric definition of the "word" is closely coupled to the message of the conclusion of the last chapter (2 Tim 3:16–17).[11] However, the charge is to proclaim the message of God and its truthful teachings, not merely Scripture alone but the message of Christ.[12] Although Paul's charge can and should encompass Scripture to fulfill the imperatives that proceed, the weight of the charge is upon the message of Christ. Charles Simeon declared, "[The preacher] is not at liberty to amuse the people with the fancies and conceits of men but must declare simply the mind and will of God."[13] Simeon charges that the preacher's emphatic declaration must rest upon the authority and sufficiency of Scripture.

Therefore, the proclamation of the gospel of Jesus is the ministry that must exist within a Christian community. The command to preach stands as the definitive call to Christian ministry.[14] Paul is commanding the emboldened proclamation of the saving gospel of Jesus the word of God, the message of truth, and the words of faith culminating in the message of the gospel (1 Tim 4:5–6, 14; 2 Tim 2:9, 15; Titus 1:3, 2:5). Therefore, the five aorist imperatives in verse 2 are concerned with the faithful presentation of

9. Black, *Read New Testament Greek*, 186.

10. Lea and Griffin, *1 Timothy, 2 Timothy, and Titus*, 243.

11. Mounce, *Pastoral Epistles*, 572.

12. Knight, *Pastoral Epistles*, 453.

13. Simeon, *2 Timothy to Hebrews*, 76–77.

14. Hughes and Chapell, *1 & 2 Timothy and Titus*, 244.

the gospel and the necessity to respond. In contrast, the four imperatives later in verse 5 concern themselves with Timothy's personal ministry faithfulness. Ultimately, Paul's urging of Timothy to preach the word and the gospel was foremost on Paul's mind—his logical progression of preaching to defend against heresy was rooted in the truthfulness of the gospel.

The remainder of the aorist imperatives flow directly from preaching the word. The words *reprove*, *rebuke*, and *exhort* were used by philosophers and moralists to describe the responsibilities of a classical grammarian.[15] Paul encouraged Timothy to strive to be a good teacher by staying closely coupled to the gospel. It is vitally important to note that the weight of Paul's command rests on "his appearing" (v. 1). The judgment to come when Christ appears conjures seriousness, and Christ's appearance connotes a glorious event, but both demand urgency. In a very real sense, Christ's kingdom is a present reality, yet Paul emphasized judgment, signaling the beginning of his kingdom with his return.[16]

One issue lies in the second aorist imperative, "be ready" (v. 2). Timothy understood this imperative in one of two contexts: the readiness of the hearers or his readiness for the task of his ministry. First, let's consider this from the position of the preacher. The presence of "in season and out of season" identifies the force of the exhortation toward Timothy as culminating in the idea of "always being ready."[17] John Chrysostom declared, "Let it always be thy season, not only in peace and security, and when sitting in the Church."[18]

Second, the verb can also mean to continue in an activity despite presumed opposition. Simeon advocated that the intention here is to emphasize the hearer's responsibility.[19] Richard Lenski noted that the charge is to herald the gospel whether or not the message seemed favorable: "The Word knows no difference as to [*kairoi*] or seasons; it is proper for all seasons, everlastingly in season; there is never a time in which it is not needed."[20] Additionally, the subjective and objective positions of the charge illuminate

15. Collins, *1 & 2 Timothy*, 269.

16. Lea and Griffin, *1 Timothy, 2 Timothy, and Titus*, 242.

17. Hervey, *II Timothy*, 57.

18. John Chrysostom, *Homilies on the Second Epistle to Timothy* 9 (*NPNF*[1] 13:510).

19. Simeon, *2 Timothy to Hebrews*, 78.

20. Lenski, *Interpretation of St. Paul's Epistles*, 854.

both interpretations as possibilities, but they ultimately work toward the same goal—preaching the word.[21]

Moreover, examining the parable of the sower supports the latter position. Essentially, the sower spread seed without regard to the soil upon which it fell (Matt 13:3–9). Linguistically, the subordinate command of "being ready" reinforces the importance of the first and primary command—preaching the word. In either respect, the emphasis on being ready is toward the end of preaching the gospel. The significance of Paul's phrase has as much to do with the agrarian culture of seasons of planting as it does with the work of ministry. Paul commended Timothy for the parallels in the faithful spreading of the seeds of the gospel despite the "season" around him. Where a planter is prepared solely for the planting season, Paul was commanding Timothy toward an ever-present attitude toward gospel proclamation.

The following three imperatives may very well refer to intellect, conscience, and volition (the mind, the emotions, and the will).[22] The whole of what makes a person is wrapped up in the individual's mind, emotions, and will. Therefore, the charge to Timothy is to speak the life of the light of the gospel to the whole person. This serves as a holistic application of the gospel to the very soul of man.

First, Paul commands Timothy to *reprove*. Paul means refuting error by reasoned argument. The term *reprove* is used against one who continues in sin (Matt 18:15, 1 Tim 5:20), for correcting an opponent (Titus 1:9, 13), and as one of the duties that must be performed with all authority (Titus 2:15). Considering this, it is appropriate to consider the use of *reprove* here as containing a similar range of meaning.[23] Paul established the truth by preaching the word, considering error as a means of reproving. Reproving then serves as instruction of the intellect—to change the mind through the illumination of truth. Jesus implored God the Father to "sanctify them in the truth; Your word is truth" (John 17:17). The charge then is to oppose lies of false teachings with the truth of the message of the person and work of Christ. In the message of Christ, truth reigns.

Second, Paul commanded Timothy to *rebuke*. The word *rebuke* holds more authority than *reprove*, indicating declaration and not the persuasion

21. Mounce, *Pastoral Epistles*, 573.

22. Lea and Griffin, *1 Timothy, 2 Timothy, and Titus*, 243.

23. Knight, *Pastoral Epistles*, 452.

of argument.[24] The word *rebuke* occurs twenty-nine times in the New Testament, yet only here does Paul use this term. Mounce pointed out that Jesus' rebuke of demons uses the term.[25] The implication appears to be a conviction of the sinner's conscience. Sharpness of a rebuke strikes at the heart of the hearer. This is the aspect of the word of God piercing "as far as the division of soul and spirit, of both joints and marrow, and able to judge the thoughts and intentions of the heart" (Heb 4:12). Charles Simeon articulated, "If there be any sins committed, he must 'rebuke' them; and, if need be, with sharpness and severity too."[26]

Third, Paul commanded Timothy to *exhort*, or "call to one's side." In this instance, the root of *exhort* drives toward a more profound understanding—to summon or call. To *exhort* is a more suitable rendering than *encourage*.[27] The importance of this is seen in Paul's charge to summon or to call. In connection with the command to preach, Timothy calls people to repentance. Paul's charge calls them to live out the gospel in a life of righteousness.[28] A. G. Sertillanges asserted that "every truth is life" and that truth is "a way leading to the end of man," therefore proclaiming that the gospel leads to life as "the gospel speaks."[29] Essentially, Paul's point is that reproof without grace, rebuke without instruction, and exhortation without biblical expectation leave the root of the error unscathed. Paul demonstrated his effectual dependence upon the Holy Spirit, knowing the importance of tethering the gospel to the intellect, the conscience, and the will.

The structure of Paul's writing here seems to have three sections: the charge of Timothy for treatment of the word of the gospel; the reason for the charge to preach the word; and finally, the internal charge to Timothy to guard his character in light of the gospel message he proclaims. The first section begins with the solemn charge with the five aorist imperatives on handling preaching the word (2 Tim 4:1–2). Ultimately, Jesus is ascribed the privileges reserved for God.[30]

24. Hervey, *II Timothy*, 57.

25. Mounce, *Pastoral Epistles*, 574.

26. Simeon, *2 Timothy to Hebrews*, 77.

27. Kelly, *Pastoral Epistles*, 206.

28. Mounce, *Pastoral Epistles*, 574.

29. Sertillanges, *Intellectual Life*, 13.

30. See Daniel L. Akin, "Mystery of Godliness Is Great," in Köstenberger and Wilder, *Entrusted with the Gospel*, 151.

### *Stand Against Heresy*

In 2 Tim 4:3–4, Paul addressed the heresy of which Timothy is to take caution. The transitional *for* demonstrated in this following section provides the reason for the previous charge.[31] It stands as the transition to the "so what" of what Paul had established. Paul admonished the theological error pervasive within the church at Ephesus. He makes a dark allusion to errant teachings and warns Timothy that the future will only intensify the present symptoms.[32] This serves to reinforce what Paul previously declared when he said, "But evil people and impostors will proceed from bad to worse, deceiving and being deceived" (2 Tim 3:13). Therefore, within this section are the fifth and sixth references to the gospel.

Additionally, amid identifying the teaching error within the church at Ephesus, Paul remained committed to his initial command to Timothy to "preach the word." His focus is on the hearers and not the false teachers.[33] The multiple false teachings contrast with Paul's singularly focused message: the gospel of Jesus.[34] The word of God, which Paul commended Timothy to preach, becomes a point of contention. When Paul said, "They will not endure," he addressed those who grow weary of hearing the gospel. Instead, they turn to false teaching to "have their ears tickled." Instead of following godly teachers, Paul cautions Timothy that some Christians will follow teachers who tell them what they want to hear. Regarding their drift, Paul argued that the audience would find the content of the gospel and the demands of Christ distasteful and would turn to what they believed would satiate them more.[35] Ever present in Paul's writing to Timothy is the allusion to his confidence: "So faith comes from hearing, and hearing by the word of Christ" (Rom 10:17) through his emphasis upon the command to "preach the word."

### *Fulfill the Ministry*

In the final verse of Paul's gospel-focused charge to Timothy (v. 5), he concluded with his last four imperatives: be sober, endure hardship, do

31. Knight, *Pastoral Epistles*, 452.
32. Kelly, *Pastoral Epistles*, 206.
33. Mounce, *Pastoral Epistles*, 575.
34. Collins, *1 & 2 Timothy*, 270.
35. Lea and Griffin, *1 Timothy, 2 Timothy, and Titus*, 244.

the work of an evangelist, and fulfill the ministry. Just as the first five imperatives encompassed the proclamation of the word, these last four commended Timothy for faithfulness in his ministry execution. It is important to note that these aorist imperatives are descriptors of Timothy's character while proclaiming the gospel. Moreover, Paul's treatment of the action is independent of the parts or the time, but in this instance, these attributes will happen in accordance with preaching the word.

First, Paul commanded Timothy to *be sober*, implying being "well-balanced." The historical view of the charge to steer clear of heretical teaching was thought to regard the consumption of wine.[36] Rather, being sober is a caution to clarity of mind and sound judgment, not being blinded and carried away by error and worldly opinions. Being sober-minded, therefore, connotes being sound in reason and understanding of the message of Christ. I would contend that this stands as a charge to Timothy and to us, to maintain a certainty and clarity in the gospel. The first pastor I worked with used to tell me, "The call to ministry is the call to prepare for ministry." This stands as the call to be sober, to be prepared and ready.

Second, Paul commanded Timothy to *endure hardship*, giving light to Paul's calling for him to share in the suffering of the gospel (2 Tim 1:8). The certainty of Paul's declaration of hardships rested squarely on his current situation, considering the impending departure addressed in verse 6: "For I am already being poured out as a drink offering, and the time of my departure has come." Ultimately, *for* confirms the call to evangelize through the preaching of the gospel.[37] Kelly clarified that Timothy was to perform the work of an evangelist and preach the gospel in contrast to "alien fables."[38]

Third, Paul commanded Timothy to *do the work of an evangelist*. Griffin and Lea ascribed the work of evangelism to Timothy's ministry, not to an office held.[39] Knight attests to how the use of *evangelist* is an indicator of Timothy as the evangelist for Ephesus and that Paul's encouragement is to continue that work.[40] Further, Barrett's observations suggested that evangelism was every believer's responsibility. He posited that the implication of a specific "office" would be inappropriate.[41]

36. Mounce, *Pastoral Epistles*, 576.
37. Heckert, *Discourse Function of Conjoiners*, 31.
38. Kelly, *Pastoral Epistles*, 207.
39. Lea and Griffin, *1 Timothy, 2 Timothy, and Titus*, 245.
40. Knight, *Pastoral Epistles*, 452.
41. Barrett, *Epistle to the Romans*, 27.

Finally, Paul commanded Timothy to *fulfill his ministry*. Paul identified the imperatives of pastoral ministry encapsulated in the command to preach the word—to be ready, reprove, rebuke, and exhort (2 Tim 4:2)—and ultimately of pastoral character in executing his duty—to be sober, endure hardship, and do the work of an evangelist (2 Tim 4:5). This connection demonstrates that the command to "preach the word" is intrinsically connected to the command "do the work of an evangelist" as the culmination of how to "fulfill" or "make complete" the ministry. Hughes and Chapell stated, "The gospel was to be Timothy's lifework to 'do the work of an evangelist.'"[42]

Paul asserted, "Fulfill your ministry," showing the complete pastoral ministry identified in his thoughts. To Paul, the church's ministry incorporates preaching through evangelism. Chiao Ek Ho elucidated, "Preaching the gospel lies at the heart of Paul's concern for the church."[43] It is crucial to note that Timothy was not called an evangelist but rather called to the work of evangelism—an essential distinction given the passage's context. Therein, one can see that the pastor's responsibility in preaching and evangelism is interrelated toward the same end—proclaiming the gospel.

The spirit of the text is the author-intended "feel" grounded in the genre.[44] The sermon preached should reflect the genre of the text—not only in structure but also in the feel of the literature. As exegesis gives way to the excavation of the history and the structure, the preacher should keep a watchful eye on the overall feel of the genre. Hershael W. York wrote, "At the heart of the doctrine of the inerrancy of Scripture lies this conviction: through the biblical authors transmitted the revelation they received from God in their vocabulary and through their own experience, the Holy Spirit enabled them to do without human error creeping in and marring the message."[45]

The ultimate purpose of preaching is to stand before people and declare the message of God as revealed through his word. The transformative power in the believer's life lies in God's revealed word. The issue lies in accurately communicating God's intended meaning. Paul recognized the

42. Hughes and Chapell, *1 & 2 Timothy and Titus*, 247.

43. See Chiao Ek Ho, "Mission in the Pastoral Epistles," in Köstenberger and Wilder, *Entrusted with the Gospel*, 261.

44. Smith, "Essential Elements."

45. Hershael W. York, "Communication Theory and Text-Driven Preaching," in Akin et al., *Text-Driven Preaching*, 229.

weight and authority of Scripture wrapped up in the word originating with God himself.[46] This careful examination of 2 Tim 4:1–5 demonstrates the usefulness of the text-driven paradigm—substance, structure, spirit, and summons—as a practical road map to accomplish the expositional task.

## Conclusion

Paul's focus begins with the truth of the word and, here again, culminates toward that end. He urged Timothy to preach the gospel—the work of the evangelist. Although Timothy may not have been a grace-gifted evangelist, as seen in Eph 4, he was called to the work of an evangelist—to proclaim the gospel. Paul expected Timothy to be sober in judgment, bearing suffering with patience, and to assume the preaching of the gospel as Paul was about to depart. Therefore, just as Paul admonished Timothy to "preach the word" (2 Tim 4:2) and "do the work of an evangelist" (v. 5), so should preachers today. D. Martyn Lloyd-Jones succinctly asserted, "The primary task of the Church and the Christian minister is the preaching of the Word of God."[47]

The principle of the whole ministry of the church encapsulates the ministry of the word. The word of God should permeate the whole of ministry, especially the pulpit ministry. This preaching principle aligns with Paul's declaration in 1 Timothy. John Stott declared,

> Paul wrote in 1 Timothy 3:15 that the Church is "the pillar and foundation of the truth." The two words he used are instructive. The Church is both the foundation (or buttress) of the truth on the one hand, and the pillar of the truth on the other. Foundations and buttresses hold a building firm; pillars hold it high, thrusting it aloft for people to see. This suggests both the apologetic task and the evangelistic task of the Church. For, as the foundation or buttress of the truth, the Church must hold it firm and defend it against heretics, so that the truth remains steadfast and immovable. But, as the pillar of the truth, the Church must hold it high, making it visible to the world, so that people may see it and believe. So the Bible needs the Church to protect it and to spread it.[48]

46. Adam, *Speaking God's Words*, 105.
47. Lloyd-Jones, *Preaching and Preachers*, 26.
48. Stott, *God's Word*, 43.

He drew to the front the necessity of the twofold ministry of the word: (1) build the church, and (2) defend the truth against heresy. This view holds in tension the minister's work in Paul's further charge to preach the word.

Furthermore, Paul sets an expectation of response, so the hearer should respond to the proclamation of the word. The charge for believers is to stand faithfully upon the truth of the gospel. Paul charged Timothy to preach the word, expecting the hearers to submit to the truth of Scripture. The charge is in the proclamation of the word, responding in humility to the reproving, rebuking, and exhortation that flows from the message of Christ against the false doctrines of false teachers. Everyone has some aspects of lousy theology that the truth of Scripture must correct. Humility is how one responds when Scripture illuminates errors within theology. The corrective then rests on the faithful proclamation of the word and the expectation of a response to that proclamation.

To proclaim the gospel in preaching is to make known the great mysteries of God revealed in God's chosen mode of revelation—the person of Christ and the Holy Scriptures. It is not an accident that Paul commands Timothy to "preach the word" immediately after he commends him to press on in the truth of the gospel. Paul wrote,

> You, however, continue in the things you have learned and become convinced of, knowing from whom you have learned them, and that from childhood you have known the sacred writings which are able to give you the wisdom that leads to salvation through faith which is in Christ Jesus. All Scripture is inspired by God and profitable for teaching, for reproof, for correction, for training in righteousness; so that the man of God may be adequate, equipped for every good work. (2 Tim 3:14–17)

Paul demonstrated three key principles of a theology of preaching in this short excerpt of Scripture: (1) the "sacred writings" can give wisdom that leads to salvation because they reveal Jesus Christ; (2) these Scriptures are inspired by God himself and serve as his divine revelation of himself and his redemptive plan; (3) God's revelation teaches, reproves, corrects, and trains in righteousness. Scripture—by the power of the Holy Spirit—imbues the hearer with wisdom toward the end of redemption in Christ. This wisdom, often demonstrated by Paul in his reasoning (Acts 17:17, 24:25, 26:28), reveals the apologia of the gospel that he so passionately proclaimed. Randy Newman referred to this as pre-evangelism: "Pre-evangelism is part of the task of sowing. All that preparatory work is vital if we want to see our seeds bear gospel fruit."[49]

Additionally, 2 Tim 4:1–5 illuminates the lordship of Christ and his imminent return. The eternal hope of salvation rests in Christ alone, and the gospel message paves the road to salvation through the person and the work of Christ. Charles Spurgeon advised, "From every text in Scripture, there is a road toward the great metropolis, Christ. I have never found a text that does not have a road to Christ in it."[50] The charge to the unbeliever rests in the fact that Christ has come, and the way to salvation has come by his gospel enterprise. Drummond attested that accepting the gospel transforms the person's interaction with the Holy Spirit. To those far from Christ, he asserted that the Spirit is "the Accuser," but through pierced conscience and profession of faith, the Spirit becomes "the Advocate."[51] Therefore, preaching the word convicts of sin, and the charge in response is deciding for or against Christ—the work of an evangelist. Newman attested, "Evangelism occurs at the intersection of the human and the divine, the natural and the supernatural, the practical and the impossible. God calls timid Timothy to 'do the work of an evangelist.' Then God provides what no human can—opening up blind eyes, softening hardened hearts, and drawing people to himself."[52]

Paul's appeal to the preaching of the word demonstrates the impact of rhetorical persuasion of the hearer through the mind (Timothy reproves their understanding through the gospel, or the *logos*), the emotions (Timothy rebukes their emotions through the gospel, or the *pathos*), and the volition (Timothy exhorts their will through the gospel, or the *ethos*). Paul commends the gospel to the whole person—the mind, emotions, and will. He therefore demonstrates the response to the gospel within the complexity of the summons of the text, as established through his use of the gospel. This call of the summons of the text is displayed in a call to salvation, both expressed through justification and sanctification. The expectation of obedience in response to the gospel is explicit—the summons of the text toward justification is surrender to Christ, while its sanctifying call is found in correcting heretical teaching and salvation through the work of

49. Newman, *Mere Evangelism*, 30.

50. From "Christ Precious to Believers," in Spurgeon, *New Park Street Pulpit*, 5:140.

51. Drummond, *Word of the Cross*, 179.

52. Newman, *Mere Evangelism*, 19.

evangelism—the call to the mind, the call to the emotions, and the call to volition through obedience.

# CHAPTER 7

# The Persuasive Art of Preaching

The goal of any argument in an expositional sermon should be to persuade the hearer toward a deeper understanding of and dependence upon Christ. Adrian Rogers asserted, "You are preaching for a verdict. There is something you want your people to know, do, and believe."[1] Therefore, the foundation of preaching rests upon rhetoric—the classical art of persuasion. However, not all preachers are students of rhetoric. Instead, the tools of rhetoric have shaped the history of preaching, and all preachers employ rhetoric—knowingly or unknowingly. Employing rhetoric can account for both understanding and misunderstanding, only as it seeks to analyze the tiniest meaningful units of language that are structured, and how their form changes when joined with others.[2] The greatest sermons in history all have a common thread. Historically powerful sermons have demonstrated four distinct characteristics: the preacher and his audience, the sermon's content, the form of the discourse, and the preservation of sermons.[3]

Nevertheless, one of the greatest struggles throughout the centuries in employing persuasion in preaching lies in the source of the argument. The persuasion of the sermon must be rooted in and rest upon the *exegesis* of the text and not be prone to extraneous pontifications. Persuasion in expository preaching rests primarily upon expounding the text itself. The persuasive nature of rhetorical functions is subordinate to the meaning and message of the text of Scripture. Looking at consistency of meaning,

1. Rogers, *Preaching for Impact*, 76.
2. Richards, *Philosophy of Rhetoric*, 9–10.
3. Dargan, *From the Apostolic Fathers*, 36.

I. A. Richards noted, "Preeminently what the [context theorem of meaning] would discourage, if a passage means one thing, it cannot at the same time mean another and an incompatible thing."[4] The text has a distinct meaning; the preacher must seek God's intended meaning. Karl Barth asserted, "Proclamation of the Word can be no more than a simple repetition of the witness that is given to us in Scripture; the task takes on a broader dimension inasmuch as we have to follow this way of the witness into the present."[5] Fundamentally, the preacher must identify the main idea and the supporting points within the passage of Scripture and present the argument to the congregation.

## Historical Foundations of Rhetorical Persuasion in Preaching

The foundation of any persuasive argument lies within the rhetorical appeal of the speaker. The first functional definition of rhetoric arose from Aristotle's *On Rhetoric* in the fourth century BC.[6] Classical rhetoric spans three distinct types—forensic, political, and ceremonial—that emerged from Greek democracy. However, later rhetoricians expanded these types to encompass all forms of communication.[7] This expansion of types is due in part to the defining characteristic of rhetoric: persuasion.[8] Five distinct stages make up classical rhetoric. These stages are the canons of rhetoric and consist of invention, arrangement, style, memory, and delivery.

This chapter examines the foundations of rhetoric in the history of preaching, illuminating the historical use of rhetorical persuasion. It will summarize the role of rhetorical persuasion in the history of preaching by examining (1) select apostles' use of rhetoric, (2) select patristic preachers' use of rhetoric, and (3) select Reformation preachers' use of rhetoric as a cursory examination. This examination lays the foundation for arguing for the summons by developing the historical precedent for persuasion and the preacher's expectation of a response from the congregation.

4. Richards, *Philosophy of Rhetoric*, 38.

5. Barth, *Homiletics*, 111.

6. Historically, rhetoric was seen in education and public affairs as early as the fifth century BC, but it was formalized through Aristotle.

7. Bizzell and Herzberg, *Rhetorical Tradition*, 3.

8. Aristotle, *On Rhetoric* 1.2 (37).

Within the invention, the speaker builds his argument from what he knows to persuade the listener.[9] A. C. Baird argued that invention is the "investigation, analysis, and grasp of subject matter."[10] To this extent, logical proofs move the audience toward the speaker's position. Aristotle's internal proofs in rhetoric are known as the trivium of rhetoric—*logos*, *ethos*, and *pathos*. These internal proofs support the speaker's defense and form the foundation of all persuasion. In Aristotle's estimation, *logos* is what the speaker is saying, *ethos* is the reputation or character of the speaker, and *pathos* is the appeal to emotions.

Although regarded as primarily an approach to civic discourse, Aristotle's *On Rhetoric* does contain facets of the metaphysical.[11] These aspects of Aristotle look to the essence of being. Rhetoric then serves to persuade not only empirical reason but also the soul of man. R. L. Dabney further clarified that rhetoric is the art of persuasion, intending to move the hearer toward the desired result as "a practical determination of the hearer's will. . . . Rhetorical discourse should not only deal with the intellect (to produce mental conviction) but with the affections to direct the motives."[12]

Applying rhetoric to preaching has positive and negative implications. Regarding the dangers of rhetoric in preaching, David Larsen wrote, "Too much of Aristotle may indeed be problematic, but the idea of rhetoric as the application style for persuasion and the law of contradiction are good even if they emanate from a Greek pagan."[13] Therefore, preachers should apply rhetoric to preaching despite its secular origins. Regardless of the concerns surrounding rhetoric in preaching, there is a foundational connection to its use for persuasion throughout history.

## Ancient Rhetoric and the Apostles' Preaching

The role that rhetoric has played in the history of preaching is evidenced in the theological convictions of said preaching. Since the invention of the trivium of rhetoric, it has played a crucial role in preaching.[14] Over the centuries, preachers have endeavored to refine the impact of preaching

9. McCroskey, *Introduction to Rhetorical Communication*, 188.

10. Baird, *Rhetoric*, 15.

11. Kennedy, *Classical Rhetoric*, 75.

12. Dabney, *Evangelical Eloquence*, 233.

13. Larsen, *Company of the Preachers*, 2:555.

14. Bizzell and Herzberg, *Rhetorical Tradition*, 175.

through persuasion. As evidenced in the New Testament, the Holy Spirit charged the apostles with the kerygma—the message proclaimed and the act of proclamation. It is noteworthy to see that the New Testament authors recorded the preaching in Greek for a Greek audience. This audience would have understood the role of rhetorical oratory principles or, at a minimum, been educated by Greek grammarians—teachers who specialized in language and texts.

Moreover, the speeches of the apostles closely parallel the rhetorical style of the Greco-Roman historiography of the time. Robert Mounce asserted, "To 'preach' involved dialectical entanglement with the opposition. Mere announcement of a historical event would not suffice. Hence, arguing, testifying, pleading, and proving—all were necessary parts of early preaching."[15] The earliest writings in the New Testament serve as an apologia for the risen Christ. These defenses were often in direct response to the political oppression and subsequent persecution of the Christian population.[16]

Modern homilists recognize the apostles' use of rhetoric as foundational to their preaching. The preaching of the apostles in the New Testament was rhetorical but effectively classified as missionary sermons.[17] The apostles intended to persuade people of Christ's messiahship—first to the Jew and then to the gentile (Rom 1:17b). The apostles' approach to preaching must guide the modern preacher. Rhetorical persuasion serves as a common thread in their primitive kerygma. At its core, this kerygma that the apostles espoused was both a declaration and an appeal. Richard Longenecker explained, "What [the apostles] were conscious of was interpreting the Scriptures from a Christocentric perspective, in conformity with the exegetical teaching and example of Jesus, along Christological lines."[18] They declared the message of the risen Savior Jesus Christ and appealed—through dependence upon the Holy Spirit—to the hearers to respond.

## The Preaching of Peter: A Case Study

Peter provides the first example in the book of Acts of apostolic preaching and its uses of rhetoric. Ancient orators of the day would stand to face

15. Mounce, *Essential Nature*, 56.
16. Bizzell and Herzberg, *Rhetorical Tradition*, 431.
17. Kennedy, *Classical Rhetoric*, 155.
18. Longenecker, *Biblical Exegesis*, 103.

the crowd, so Peter, "taking his stand with the eleven, raised his voice and declared to them" (Acts 2:14a). Peter's sermon at Pentecost stands as an example of the forensic rhetoric he employs in his discourse to defend Christ in the following strategy: he defends the resurrection evidenced by the Holy Spirit (vv. 14–21); he defends Jesus as Lord and Messiah (vv. 22–36); and then he offers the hope of the gospel (vv. 37–38). Peter established key statements to defend against the accusation of being drunk. He argued for the significance of God making Jesus both "Lord" and "Christ," and for Jesus being attested to the crowd by miracles, for which they ultimately crucified him.[19] Finally, he declared how they should respond.

Peter's sermon employed the Jewish *midrashic* approach to interpreting Old Testament passages, thereby presuming the inerrancy and consistency of Scripture.[20] He anchored his argument in the self-interpreting nature of Scripture. His sermon in Acts 2 contains the exhortation to embrace the truth of the gospel message, which was sufficient to "pierce their hearts" by the power of the Holy Spirit. Graeme Goldsworthy espoused, "It is remarkable in Acts 2 that Peter's sermon contained no appeal. The appeal came from the congregation: 'What should we do?' It was the power and clarity of the gospel message that impressed them with the need to do something about it."[21]

## *Scripture Reveals God*

Let us briefly look at Peter's sermon at Pentecost in Acts chapter 2. The theology woven through Acts rests upon Jesus' own declaration when he said, "You shall be My witnesses both in Jerusalem, and in all Judea and Samaria, and even to the remotest part of the earth" (Acts 1:8). With this in mind, Lukan authorship is in concert between the Gospel of Luke and Acts. In his Gospel, Luke ascribed to Jesus Christ the title *Savior* in recounting his birth (Luke 2:11). Further, Jesus himself inaugurated his public ministry, proclaiming the fulfillment of the prophet Isaiah (Luke 4:16–21). Although the salvific terminology is not used, the words cited indicate the gracious, saving character of his message.[22] Moreover, as God graciously appointed his salvation, there are allusions to the "year of Jubilee," the year appointed

19. Soards, *Speeches in Acts*, 36.

20. Bray, *Biblical Interpretation*, 57.

21. Goldsworthy, *Preaching the Whole Bible*, 95.

22. Peterson, *Acts of the Apostles*, 66.

in Lev 25 to liberate, which is now made tangible through the work of Christ.[23] Although it is a theological history, the book of Acts records God's active work to fulfill his promises and his purpose for mankind.[24] Acts reveals the coming of the Messiah and the intended purpose of the arrival of the Messiah: salvation. Acts builds up a simple gospel message: salvation comes by no other name than Jesus, and it is brought solely by the mighty hand of God.[25] The essential parts of the apostolic kerygma stand here as the scriptural proofs concerning the dawn of the messianic age through Jesus, an emphasis on his death and resurrection, the exaltation of Jesus as Lord and Messiah, the affirmation of the work of Christ through the Holy Spirit's power in the church, the anticipation of Christ's imminent return, and ultimately a call to repentance.[26]

Looking at Peter's Pentecost sermon, we can see that it was the power of the Holy Spirit that filled Peter, encouraging him to proclaim Christ crucified. Therefore, Pentecost holds great significance in God revealing himself through Scripture—the apostolic kerygma. For first-century Jews, Pentecost announces the day of the Lord and ultimately his righteous judgment. However, Christians view Pentecost as the day of God's salvation to all who call upon his name.[27] Pentecost led to the outpouring and outworking of the Holy Spirit in and through the disciples. It stands as the culmination of God's revelation to his creation. Paul Washer wrote, "It is [in the gospel] that we find the most complete revelation of God's attributes in perfect harmony. There, his holiness and righteousness are revealed in the punishment of sin. There, his grace and mercy are revealed in the suffering of his Son in the place of his guilty people."[28] We can see this very dichotomy in Peter's Pentecost sermon, as the gospel foretold by the prophets of God is revealed. The basic structure of Acts 2:1–13 is narrative, and it acts as an introduction to his sermon. In these verses, Peter summarized God's redemption plan in action—the ministry of Christ, the death, and ultimately, his resurrection. What is significant about these three statements is that God is the primary agent in each instance. Moreover, it is worth noting that Jesus was not initiated as Lord and Messiah; instead, God revealed him as such through the

23. Marshall, *Gospel of Luke*, 184.

24. Peterson, *Acts of the Apostles*, 53.

25. Polhill, *Acts*, 55.

26. Dodd, *Apostolic Preaching*, 24–28.

27. Bruce, *Book of the Acts*, 62.

28. Washer, *Preeminent Christ*, 44.

power of the resurrection. Grant Osborne wrote, "The fact that God 'made' him to be Lord and Messiah does not mean he was not such before. Rather, it means God has demonstrated who he truly had been all along through his resurrection and the pouring out of the Spirit."[29]

### *Scripture Defends the Resurrection of Christ*

Peter's approach to the passage from Joel 2 shifts from *midrash* to *pesher*, a method of interpreting the Old Testament used by the Essenes. His focus was on ascribing the fulfillment of the prophecy in the events of the resurrection and the outpouring of the Holy Spirit. The apostles were filled with the Holy Spirit. Peter's defense begins with the integrity of his fellow apostles and quickly turns to the necessity of the resurrection. Osborne noted, "Peter presents the key to everything in verse 21: 'Everyone who calls on the name of the Lord will be saved.' For Joel, the title 'the Lord' refers to Yahweh, while for Peter it refers to Christ, implying the deity of Christ, cosmic Lord of all."[30] God's use of the phrase "pour out My Spirit on all mankind" (Joel 2:28) is understood in its context of the previous section of "poured down for you the rain" found in Joel 2:23. Both are saving works of the day of the Lord. Duane Garrett wrote, "The Bible several times associates the Holy Spirit with water or describes him metaphorically as something that can be poured out (Isa 44:3; Ezek 39:29; Zech 12:10; Rom 5:5). Joel easily turned this imagery to his advantage and created a parallel between the gift of rain and the pouring out of the Spirit."[31]

### *Scripture Exalts Christ as Lord and Messiah*

Peter drew upon the gospel and demonstrated a comprehensive kerygma—the exaltation of Christ and the call to repentance through the power of the Holy Spirit. F. F. Bruce asserted, "The miracles of Jesus were not mere 'wonders'; they were 'mighty works,' evidences of the power of God operating among the people, and 'signs' of the kingdom of God."[32] Therein lies the declaration of the kingdom of God manifest among God's people. A key

29. Osborne, *Acts*, 56–57.
30. Osborne, *Acts*, 50.
31. Garrett, *Hosea, Joel*, 367–68.
32. Bruce, *Book of the Acts*, 62.

distinction is that Peter's use of the phrase "these words" indicates what is to follow, not what he spoke (Acts 2:22).

First, Peter's assertion affirmed the words of Jesus: "The Spirit of the Lord is upon Me because He anointed Me to preach the gospel to the poor. He has sent me to proclaim release to the captives, and recovery of sight to the blind, to set free those who are oppressed, to proclaim the favorable year of the Lord" (Luke 4:18–19)[33] Jesus' use of Isa 61 provided a context in which previous passages alluded to someone coming to proclaim the good news (Isa 40:9, 41:27, and 52:7). God is the one who announced the good news through his chosen servants, the messenger of good news, as alluded to in Isa 41:27.[34]

In addition, in concert with Isa 52:7, the "good news" refers to the message of peace and salvation. Here, the gospel message proclaimed by Jesus contained elements of *soteria*. Peter's expression of kerygma demonstrated a promise closely coupled with the gospel message, resounding with purpose, inheritance, and glory still to be revealed.[35] Darrell Bock declared, "The only way to be delivered from the day is to call upon the name of the Lord and thereby seek God's salvation."[36] Seeking God's mercy in the face of judgment and adversity is a recurring theme in the Old Testament. Peter leveraged this understanding to point to Christ.

Second, Peter established the validity of Jesus' claim through the attestation of the miracles he performed. Therefore, Peter declared that Jesus Christ is who he professed, and the evidence is irrefutable. David Peterson announced, "Such evidence might simply lead to the conclusion that he was 'a prophet, powerful in word and deed before God and all the people' (Luke 24:19). However, Peter proceeds to identify him specifically as the promised Messiah."[37]

Finally, Peter provided the accusation of Christ being "delivered over" and "nailed to a cross by . . . godless men" (Acts 2:23), which serves a twofold purpose here. The indictment stood against Israel for handing Christ over for punishment at the hands of the Romans. It is undeniable that Peter's accusation is toward the Jewish nation for their part in handing over the Lord to be crucified at the hands of heathens—the Roman state.

33. From the record of Jesus reading from Isa 61:1.

34. Smith, *Isaiah 40–66*, 631–32.

35. See William Arnold, "Salvation," in Elwell, *Evangelical Dictionary*, 701.

36. Bock, *Acts*, 118.

37. Peterson, *Acts of the Apostles*, 145.

It is vitally important to note that this is the first appearance in the book of Acts that references God's plans and purposes. The significance of God's plans and purposes emphasizes God's sovereignty in everything that happened. Not one thing occurred that was outside of the deliberate plan and foreknowledge of God.[38] Moreover, what evil men devised was not outside the purview of God. Instead, he allowed their actions to further his ultimate goal of salvation through Christ. Newman and Nida expressed the difficulty of translating the phrase "predetermined will and foreknowledge of God."[39] However, it is vitally important to understand that God had already decided on what was to happen and revealed this truth through his prophets.

Next, Peter employs Ps 16:8–11 to defend Jesus' claims as the Messiah. Darrell Bock stated, "Peter uses the psalm because the kind of defense God gave to the psalmist is like that which Jesus received, a typological-prophetic use. God's protection and the certainty of it are the keys to the citation's tone and use."[40] Peter claimed Christ was the Messiah and appealed to Ps 16 as his scriptural proof. Ultimately, he used Ps 16 as proof that the resurrection testified to the messianic nature of Jesus.

Thus, Peter applied the psalm to Christ. His use of the psalm proved that Jesus was the Messiah.[41] F. F. Bruce wrote, "These prophetic words, Peter goes on to argue, have been fulfilled in Jesus of Nazareth and no one else; Jesus of Nazareth is, therefore, the expected Messiah."[42] Furthermore, first-century Christians understood the title "your holy one" of Acts 2:27 as explicitly referring to the messianic Son of David.[43] Thus, Peter's use of the psalms is critical in his argumentation for Jesus as the Messiah. Darrell Bock expounded, "If the psalm was ever to be connected to David, it must surely be connected even more to Christ, whom God has shown Jesus to be by this resurrection."[44] Peter looks to David and the psalm's prophetic nature to identify Jesus' messianic status, which the power of the resurrection proved.

Ultimately, Peter connected the Scripture, the Messiah, and the resurrection of Jesus. Peter's intent looked to the hope of the psalmist and

38. Peterson, *Acts of the Apostles*, 145.

39. Newman and Nida, *Acts of the Apostles*, 48.

40. Bock, *Acts*, 123.

41. Polhill, *Acts*, 114.

42. Bruce, *Book of the Acts*, 62.

43. Peterson, *Acts of the Apostles*, 149.

44. Bock, *Acts*, 129.

paralleled it to the hope revealed in Jesus through his resurrection. His use of Ps 110 highlighted a contrast between David, the holy one, and Jesus Christ himself. Referring to Peter's use of Ps 110, Newman and Nida stated, "As used in the present context, the Lord is God the Father, and my Lord refers to Jesus; by raising Jesus from the dead God made him Lord and Messiah."[45] Essentially, Peter made the transition from the resurrection of Jesus Christ to his exaltation.

He emphasized Christ's exaltation over the nations, over the Roman rule, and ultimately over the Jewish scheming. Ultimately, Acts 2:36 provides the climax to Peter's sermon. Peter now concludes where he began; Jesus testified by the Old Testament prophets, and is now exalted by God as Lord and Christ. Peter shows that Scripture reveals the character and nature of Christ.

### *The Gospel Offers Salvation*

Furthermore, the culmination of the kerygma rests upon the immediate quickening of the hearts of the hearers. Darrell Bock wrote, "The crowd is deeply impressed by Peter's words. Indeed, they are cut to the heart."[46] However, in addition to conviction cutting their hearts, Peter's call for repentance led to a complete change of heart, revealing a spiritual about-face. The call to repentance, espoused by John and Jesus, remained an essential element of the apostolic message.[47] I would be remiss if I did not mention that Peter did not initiate the call to respond. The piercing of the hearts of the men was a direct result of the proclamation of Scripture by the power of the Holy Spirit. I write this as a caution against some formulaic expectation. Seek faithfulness to Christ in preaching and submit to the leading of the Holy Spirit.

Peter appealed to the *ethos* of his message when he stated, "These men are not drunk, as you suppose, for it is only the third hour of the day" (Acts 2:15a). He then presented the *logos* of his rhetoric addressing—from Scripture—the foundation of his argument (Joel 2:28–32; Ps 16:8–11, 110:1). Finally, Peter presented the *pathos* of his argument in the deep conviction of his exhortation to his audience: "Be saved from this perverse generation" (Acts 2:40). He defended against the accusation of drunkenness, anchored

45. Newman and Nida, *Acts of the Apostles*, 57.

46. Bock, *Acts*, 129.

47. Bruce, *Book of the Acts*, 69.

his speech in Scripture, and proclaimed in the boldness of the Holy Spirit's empowerment.

## The Preaching of Paul: A Case Study

Consistent with his custom, Paul reasoned with Jews in the synagogues. In Acts 17:16–21, he dialogued (*dialegomai*) with them. The use of *dialegomai* emphasizes the importance of Paul's intention. Essentially, classical rhetoric required *dialegomai* to develop persuasion through posing questions and answering them (Socratic), establishing ideas (Platonic), or investigating truth and knowledge (Aristotelian). In Greek philosophical culture, *dialegomai* is the only means by which the *logos*, or idea, can be achieved, underscoring its chief importance.[48] The distinction between Greek philosophy and Paul's attestation of Christ's message rests in God's intrinsic truthfulness. For Paul, the New Testament usage of *dialegomai* exemplified the declaration of divine truth rather than negotiation toward truth. Ben Witherington asserted, "Luke is building up a portrait of Paul as being able to stand on equal footing with the intellectuals of his day, even in Athens. Indeed, he seems to be presenting Paul as a new Socrates."[49] Ultimately, Paul's exegesis was distinctly Christocentric and reflected the literal and typological approach to interpretation.[50]

To understand Paul's preaching approach, we must examine 1 Thess 1:5. In this text, he esteemed preaching as central to his ministry but approached his proclamation with the intent to persuade his audience. In this sense, Paul leveraged the Greco-Roman distinction between functional and decorative rhetoric to persuade his hearers to accept the gospel message. We can see that the fundamental aspects of his preaching and his appeal were through rhetoric—the *ethos*, *logos*, and *pathos*.

### *The Ethos of Preaching*

Paul appealed to his personal integrity. He drew upon his *ethos*, asserting "what kind of men we proved to be" (1 Thess 1:5c). He argues that the

48. See Gottlob Schrenk, "διαλέγομαι," in Kittel et al., *Theological Dictionary of the New Testament*, 93.

49. Witherington, *Acts of the Apostles*, 514.

50. Hinson, *Evangelization of the Roman Empire*, 195.

character of the messengers of the gospel is on full display. Paul contended it was "for [their] sake" (1 Thess 1:5d), articulating that his moral behavior was to present the gospel for their benefit. D. Michael Martin stated, "Thus Paul clearly understood that just as he sought to imitate Christ, so also he was obligated to serve as an example of the Christian life to others."[51] Paul was acutely aware of his character's influence on the receptiveness of the gospel message.

Therefore, whether or not they are text driven, the duty of every preacher is fidelity to God's word—the power of salvation. The power of the sermon rests not upon the preacher's persuasion but on the power of the Holy Spirit. H. B. Charles asserted, "A faithful preacher must be consistent. . . . Aim to be consistent. It is not enough to get it right now and then. There is a word for a man who is only faithful to his wife when you catch him right: unfaithful!"[52] Charles's comparison to an unfaithful husband clarifies the importance of the need for fidelity to God's word. The consistency and fidelity to the text hold the severest of ramifications.

Ultimately, you cannot preach what you yourself do not know. William Shakespeare understood this principle in the assertion of his character Polonius: "This above all: to thine own self be true, and it must follow, as the night the day, Thou canst not then be false to any man."[53] Herein lies the struggle of moral-therapeutic and narcissistic, optimistic, deistic preaching—they sacrifice textual fidelity on the altar of societal relevance. Much of what we have seen from pulpits has centered around moral-therapeutic deistic preaching. This modern approach to preaching seeks to water down the power of Scripture, reducing it to moral advice that resonates as self-help. It offers comfort without challenge, morality without the necessity of the gospel, grace without cost, and God without lordship.

Related to this, we find narcissistic, optimistic, deistic preaching. This preaching aims to bend Scripture to center on the self while maintaining a light, upbeat tone, acknowledging God as a vague spiritual background to the painting of life. It offers a god as a projection of the human ego, leaves us bankrupt in suffering, and ultimately mirrors a consumerist culture. Both employ Scripture to their own ends rather than allowing it to shape them. David Helm identified this type of preaching with what he called "inebriated" preaching—he expounded, "Some preachers use the Bible the way a

51. Martin, *1, 2 Thessalonians*, 60–61.

52. Charles, *On Preaching*, 117.

53. Shakespeare, *Hamlet*, act 1, scene 1, lines 78–80 (Barnet, 923).

drunk man uses a lamp post . . . more for support than for illumination."[54] The *ethos* of the faithful preacher depends upon fidelity to the intended meaning of Scripture.

## *The Logos of Preaching*

Next, Paul established the necessity of the message proclaimed—the *logos*. Paul asserted, "For our gospel did not come to you in word only" (1 Thess 1:5a). The *logos* is present in the rational proclamation of the message. However, Paul emphasized that it was more than words—evidence, power, Spirit, and conviction confirmed it. Grant Osborne stated, "'Words' and 'power' are not in contrast to one another but are interdependent, with the words of the proclamation undergirded with power."[55] Paul's allusion is twofold: (1) the literal spoken word, and (2) the literal person and work of Christ.

Expositional preachers assert that God wholly inspires the text of Scripture.[56] Paul attested that "all Scripture is inspired by God" (2 Tim 3:16a). Preaching with a view of the whole Bible depends upon the abiding conviction of Scripture's sufficiency. Goldsworthy stated, "It is vital for us to remember that our reference point is Jesus of Nazareth as he is testified to by Holy Scripture. The apostolic testimony to him shapes our approach to the Bible as a whole. This testimony necessitates the self-conscious formation of a biblical-theological approach to the unity and diversity of the Bible."[57]

Faithful text-driven exposition demands a foundation built upon the conviction that God's word is inspired, inerrant, infallible, and sufficient for mankind. There is a need for sermons to rest upon direct biblical authority.[58] A conviction of biblical authority emphasizes precision in exposition and interpretation. Determining the passage's meaning in its pericope is the first step in understanding the meaning. When the word of God saturates the preacher's heart, then the passion of the transformation

54. Helm, *Expositional Preaching*, 24.

55. Osborne, *1 & 2 Thessalonians*, 26.

56. See John Stott, "Definition of Biblical Preaching," in Robinson and Larson, *Art and Craft*, 24.

57. Goldsworthy, *Preaching the Whole Bible*, xi.

58. See Adam Hughes, "The Soul of the Evangelistic Expository Sermon," in Price, *Engage*, 449.

cannot help but exude from the sermon. This saturation is what John Owen referred to as the glory of Christ in his person. He disclosed, "When we read Scripture, we must always bear in mind that the revelation and doctrine of the person of Christ and His office are the foundation of all that we learn from the prophets and apostles. Deny this, and the Scriptures will no longer become a revelation of the glory of God in the salvation of the church."[59] Honest argumentation begins with self-reflection. To what end does the preacher aim to communicate—his glory or God's? Augustine exposed the heart of this thought when he discussed that rhetoric is for the purpose that "[good men] may fight for truth."[60] The truth of Scripture must be the immutable standard to which the man of God anchors his life. Therefore, the motivation behind textually faithful preaching must be the glory of God.

### *The Pathos of Preaching*

Unlike classical rhetoric, which strives to blend eloquence with wisdom, sacred rhetoric surrenders both to the working of the Holy Spirit through the preacher.[61] When Paul presented the gospel, it was more than just the average rhetoric of his day. Although he used the same terminology as ancient philosophers, he did not end there. His use of *power* and *conviction* (1 Thess 1:5) further elaborates how the Holy Spirit manifests himself.[62] He fully embraced and acknowledged the Holy Spirit's role in the presentation of the gospel. Paul's understanding of the sufficiency of the word, in cooperation with the power of the Holy Spirit, guided his rhetoric. Therein was the key to his presentation of the gospel. He humbly acknowledged the Holy Spirit's role and the gospel's power in his rhetoric. His first letter to the Thessalonians notably demonstrated his dependence upon the Holy Spirit. He further recognized the *logos* of preaching as the "gospel did not come . . . in word only" (1 Thess 1:5a). It was more than human words. Preaching is a coupling of the gospel's message (the *logos*) and the passionate empowerment of the Holy Spirit (the *pathos*). This coupling stirs the religious affections of the congregation to respond to the exhortation and application of the text of Scripture.

59. Owen, *Glory of Christ*, 31.

60. Augustine, *On Teaching Christianity* 4.2 (Hill, 208).

61. Augustine, *On Teaching Christianity* 4.8 (Hill, 211).

62. Bruce, *1 and 2 Thessalonians*, 14.113

Moreover, *ethos* plays a critical role in preaching. The preacher's *ethos* gives way to his *pathos*, demonstrated through how he communicates the *logos*. Thomas Sheridan asserted that when the speaker separates words from the tone, "they play the fool . . . because he uses words only and omits the use of the true signs of the passion, which are tones, looks, and gestures."[63] Ultimately, the preacher's tone further captures the emotion of the argument, revealing the preacher's *ethos*. He must recognize that it is here that the text must imbue the whole self to transmit the meaning of the text effectively.

Therefore, the passionate heart cry (*pathos*) of the preacher's very words is at the center of the persuasive argument, but words necessitate both the *ethos* and *pathos* of the speaker. The word of God must first touch the preacher's heart before he can effectually capture the passion of the message.[64] John Calvin wrote, "Scripture has its own order and plan that is more beautiful and certain than any philosophic method."[65] That order is toward the glory of God through the redemption of humanity. The person of Christ meeting humanity's ultimate need wraps up redemption. All that remains is to speak with a Spirit-filled and Christ-exalting summons of the text. John Piper asserted, "God aims to exalt Himself, not the preacher, in this affair of preaching. . . . [The supremacy of God in preaching's] outline is intentionally Trinitarian: The Goal of Preaching: The Glory of God; The Ground of Preaching: The Cross of Christ; and The Gift of Preaching: The Power of the Holy Spirit."[66]

## Conclusion

As in our examples with Peter and Paul, persuasion is a vital component of preaching. It serves to bridge the gap between the biblical truth of the text and the call to the hearer's mind, emotions, and will. Persuasion is the means by which the sermon's transmission of truth couples with the heart of the hearer, compelling them to respond to the truth through repentance, faith, and obedience. Effective preaching connects with the whole person, and the preacher must employ the trivium of rhetoric—*ethos*, *pathos*, and

63. See Thomas Sheridan, "A Course of Lectures on Elocution," in Bizzell and Herzberg, *Rhetorical Tradition*, 884.

64. Robinson, *On Biblical Preaching*, 5.

65. Calvin, *Christian Life*, 5.

66. Piper, *Supremacy of God*, 25.

*logos*—to effectively connect with the audience. Preachers must strive to appeal to the mind, the emotions, and the will through heartfelt delivery, reasoned interpretation, and conscience, grounded in the truth of the word and in dependence upon the Holy Spirit. They stand as ambassadors and heralds of God's redemptive message in Christ, woven throughout Scripture. Persuasion, then, is not manipulation—it is the Spirit-empowered art of guiding souls toward the beauty, necessity, and implications of gospel truth.

This chapter examined the foundations of rhetoric and its influence on the apostles' preaching. It paid particular attention to the historical use of rhetorical persuasion in preaching. The chapter surveyed the use of persuasion in preaching—in its various forms—from the time of the apostles through the early twentieth century. Although not an exhaustive review, common themes of truth have presented themselves regarding preaching throughout history. This examination lays the foundation for incorporating the summons of the text into the text-driven preaching model. This chapter developed the historical precedence of persuasion in preaching and the preacher's expectation of a response from the congregation.

First, the *ethos* of persuasion in preaching rests on the moral and ethical attributes of the preacher himself. Purity and holiness historically marked the preacher's character in and out of the pulpit. The implication is that the character of the modern preacher must strive toward that level of moral excellence. The *ethos* directly connects to the persuasive nature of preaching.

Next, the word of God produces the *logos* of persuasion in preaching. Bryan Chapell demonstrated that expository sermons should reflect this redemptive content from every text of Scripture.[67] The pinnacle mission of the local church is preaching God's word.[68] The implication is that the message of the modern preacher must strive toward textual faithfulness. The *logos* of the sermon is directly anchored to divine persuasion—God's words.

Finally, the *pathos* of persuasion in preaching must tether to the redemptive nature of the cross above all else. All the issues of life flow toward the gospel for healing, and the gospel impacts the world. Charles Spurgeon stated that Christ should be the central focus of the sermon. Spurgeon's argument revealed the depth of his conviction when he asserted, "I am greedy

67. Chapell, *Christ-Centered Preaching*, 285.

68. Lloyd-Jones, *Preaching and Preachers*, 27.

after witnesses for the glorious gospel of the blessed God. O that Christ crucified were the universal burden of men of God! Blessed is that ministry of which Christ is all."[69] The implication is that the passion of the modern preacher must be grounded in communion with the Holy Spirit. The Holy Spirit empowers the preacher's *pathos*, multiplying the persuasive effect of preaching.

The totality of the Scriptures rests upon God's redemptive work toward mankind. That is to say, the Bible's entirety is to reveal God's glory through his redemptive plan for mankind. Considering this truth, persuasion in the sermon should latch onto the text's call to glorify God—either by conforming more to the image of Christ or by initial faith in Christ. This book will now investigate how each passage's grammatical-historical context should reveal Christ in a Christocentric fashion.

69. From "Lecture 5: Sermons—Their Matter," in Spurgeon, *Lectures*, 1:68.

# CHAPTER 8

# The Word of God Demands a Summons

As we have seen, the text calls for a change in mind, heart, and will. Theologically, we can see that the Bible calls, time and again, for people to be transformed, renewed, and to live in a newness. Romans 12:2 describes the transformation through the renewing of the mind. The necessity of the gospel's work is on full display in this passage. Our minds are renewed as we set our sights on the gospel. The proclamation of the word of Christ over our lives renews our mind's focus. I say this because it follows that "by the mercies of God" (Rom 12:1) this transformation can take place. The convictional hope we possess is not contingent upon us but rather upon Christ as God's mercy exemplified toward us. I believe this calls for heart change. Our hearts' affections are drawn toward Christ by the mercy of God. Finally, this passage also calls for a physical response: "Present your bodies" (v. 1). We live out the intellectual and emotional transformation through our will. I believe that Paul was very intentional in his order here. He starts with God's moving and then culminates in our response. Our outworking of an inward faith is the culminating proof of our relationship with Christ. When Paul writes, "So that you may prove what the will of God is" (v. 2), he is establishing that the outworking in the hearer is evidence of the transformative power of the word proving the mercy of God at work in his saints. The call to respond to the text simply affirms the truth of the message proclaimed.

Additionally, the text calls us to be a new creation and ultimately a renewed life. Paul describes in 2 Cor 5:17 the fundamental change in identity that takes place through partaking in the gospel and identifying in Christ. If you are "in Christ," then we stand as a new creation apart from the old self. We are not merely recognized by proximity to Christ but by being "in Christ." Here, I offer three understandings of this phrase. First, it identifies that such a person belongs to Christ. They have Christ not only as savior but also equally as Lord. Second, the person could be identified as part of the body of Christ, the universal church, in communion with Christ through the blessed communion with his saints. Third, this could mean identifying with Christ in his death and resurrection.

Text-driven preaching begins with the substance of the text, letting the word itself provide the message. It then examines the structure of the text to recreate the message the original author intended. Then, text-driven preaching examines the spirit of the text to capture the "feel" established by the genre and historical context. Finally, text-driven preaching should seek the summons of the text, the call to respond to God's revelation of himself.

This chapter examines six biblical examples of encountering God and the transformations or judgments that result. I am taking liberty and stating that an encounter with God also includes the word of God. This chapter will look at Moses' countenance change (Exod 34), Aaron's sons (Lev 10), Ezra's reading from the scrolls (Neh 8), Ananias and Sapphira (Acts 5), Simon the magician (Acts 8), and finally Saul's conversion (Acts 9). The text-driven preaching model ensures preaching that is not man-centered but God-centered, echoing Paul's reminder that "all Scripture is inspired by God and profitable for teaching, for reproof, for correction" (2 Tim 3:16), and driving the church to both hear and obey the living word.

## The Gospel Method

Before we begin with the examples, let me offer an approach to identifying the connection between the summons of the text and the text's substance, structure, and spirit. It begins by recognizing that the connection to Jesus is as much about his attributes as about his redemptive work. Basically, the person of Christ leads to the work of Christ—the gospel. Here, the preacher can take any passage and, in its original substance, structure, and spirit, begin to see which aspect of Christ is being revealed. In 1986, video game developer Konami ported the arcade game *Gradius*. However, the game was too challenging to beat, so Kazuhisa Hashimoto developed a cheat code to allow for easier development testing. This became known as the Konami Code because it was added to every subsequent Konami game. Utilizing a similar concept, the *Gospel Method* (see figure 1) has been devised to facilitate identifying the Christ connection of a given passage. The connection to Christ, and therefore the gospel, resides in both the work and person of Christ as revealed throughout Scripture. The *Gospel Method* helps to identify how the summons of the text connects with the main idea of the text. It breaks down as follows:

**Figure 8.1: The *Gospel Method* for theological reflection of the summons.**

Employing the *Gospel Method* enables thinking theologically about the person and work of Christ as revealed in each pericope. This does not stand as an all-encompassing rule but rather serves as a guide to the greater implications of God's revelation in the text. First, the *A* reminds us of Christ's preexistent and divine nature, his role within the Trinity, and even his sovereign role in creation. The down arrow reminds us of Christ's incarnation into the world. The right arrow reminds us of Christ's humanity and sinless life. The cross, *B*, and up arrow symbolize the centrality of the gospel outlined in 1 Cor 15. This represents the death, burial, and resurrection of Jesus. The up-right arrow reminds us of his assent to the right hand of the Father, the reign of Christ, and his lordship. Finally, the down-right arrow symbolizes the promised return.

## The Revelation of God Elicits a Response

I will boldly make a declaration that any revelation of God, primarily through the preaching of God's word, demands a response. When confronted with the truth of the God of the universe, we must each decide to embrace it wholeheartedly or turn away, effectively rejecting it. Preaching must stand in such a place. If a preacher faithfully proclaims the text, the summons of the text will demand upon the hearer a change, through justification or sanctification. For illustrative purposes, I am providing a series of examples from Scripture of responses to the truth about God. The first three are from a positive perspective, and the last three are from a negative one. To avoid belaboring the point, I will refrain from an exposition and focus on a more pastoral approach, letting this serve as a high-level overview of these stories. I will look to the plain reading of the text without seeking the expositional approach I am fond of.

## An Encounter Resulting in Countenance Change

First, we will look at an example of Moses and his countenance change from Exod 34. Moses encountered God to the extent that his face shone, and the people were afraid of him. The text reads,

> It came about, when Moses was coming down from Mount Sinai (and the two tablets of the testimony were in Moses' hand as he was coming down from the mountain), that Moses did not know that the skin of his face shone because of his speaking with Him. So when Aaron and all the sons of Israel saw Moses, behold, the skin of his face shone, and they were afraid to approach him. (Exod 34:29–30)

This example employs the literal encounter with God. Moses literally encountered the Lord on Mount Sinai. The physical response to the glory of God was evidenced in his face.

### *The Substance*

The substance of this passage reveals that God confirms Moses' encounter through the supernatural radiance of his face. As such, a genuine encounter with God (and his word) should leave an indelible mark upon us. The context suggests that Moses ascended Mount Sinai to meet with the Lord and that the result was a change in his countenance. This change illustrates for us the impact of God's holiness on us. There is a transformative power of the Lord and how it impacts us. There are a couple of parallels that we can draw regarding modern preaching and the account of Moses on Sinai. First, God's holiness is on display every time we preach the text. Scripture reveals God to his creation. As such, far greater than the felt needs of the congregation is the transformational power of God's holiness, the jewel of the passage.

## *The Structure*

The structure of the text stands as the narrative of Exod 34:29–35. In the midst of the larger narrative of Israel's rebellion, we find a reminder of the everlasting nature of God's covenant with Israel. In the previous section, we find Moses bringing new tablets to the Lord (vv. 1–9) and the covenant renewed with God (vv. 10–28). The text's structure can be seen in four movements. First, Moses comes down from Sinai after meeting with the Lord (v. 29). Next, Israel reacts in fear of Moses due to his countenance radiating the glory of the Lord (vv. 30–31). Then, Moses communicated the commands of the Lord to the people (v. 32). Finally, Moses employed the veil to mediate the glory of the Lord while being before the people (vv. 33–35). An example breakdown of the structure is as follows:

1. Moses comes down from the mountain (v. 29).
2. Israel reacts to Moses' face (vv. 30–31).
3. Moses communicates God's commands (v. 32).
4. The mediation of the veil over Moses' face when before the assembly (vv. 33–35).

## *The Spirit*

The spirit of the text reveals the somber importance of the glory of God. Also, we can see the impact of the text on God's church. Mark Dever wrote, "The most important aspect of the church's purpose is the glory of God. In the Old Testament, God created a people for the glory of his name. Even when he saved them from the result of their own sin, he saved them for the glory of his own name."[1] The immediate example of this is found just a few pages after Moses' encounter with God on Sinai and his resulting change in countenance. The Israelites made for themselves a golden calf to worship. Moses interceded with God on behalf of Israel. However, his focus is centrally focused on the glory of the Lord. Moses was concerned with how the Egyptians would look at God for bringing the Israelites out into the wilderness simply to kill them. God's glory was at stake, and Moses answered the call.

1. Dever, *Church*, 76.

Returning to Moses' countenance change, we see a call to see Christ in this story. The radiance of Moses' face would eventually fade, and he would die. However, Paul would reference Moses' fading glory with the permanence of the glory revealed through Christ. We, like Moses, "are being transformed into the same image from glory to glory" (2 Cor 3:18). Once again, Dever has succinctly stated, "The holiness of the church describes God's declaration concerning his people as well as the Spirit's progressive work. After all, the church is the dwelling place of the Holy Spirit."[2] Through the summons of the text, we should encounter God. That encounter should call us to change. Authentic encounters with the text illuminate God's presence, call for visible fruit, and allow the preacher to mediate God's glory. On full display in this story is the awe-inspiring holiness of God.

### *The Summons*

The summons of the text aims to anchor to the true proposition of God revealed. What the text declares about God should evoke in our minds, emotions, and will a charge toward God. As the text states, "Draw near to God, and He will draw near to you. Cleanse your hands, you sinners; and purify your hearts, you double-minded" (Jas 4:8). For the nonbeliever, seeing God demands falling upon the mercy of God in salvation. We need to be justified before a holy God, and for that, we need a mediator to behold God's glory without being consumed. That mediator is Jesus Christ. For the believer, holiness is not something we foster within ourselves but the direct result of genuine communion with God. This communion begins with daily submission to the lordship of Christ. Fealty to Christ produces communion with God; the result of which is the fruit of the Spirit in our lives as the Holy Spirit transforms us. Greater sanctification comes through knowing God, which can only be done through his revelation in his word.

## An Encounter Revealing Man's Disobedience

A negative encounter is depicted in the tragic story of Nadab and Abihu in Lev 10. Nadab and Abihu were sons of Aaron and served with Aaron as priests. As the story unfolds, they "offered strange fire before the Lord." The text reads,

2. Dever, *Church*, 16.

> Now Nadab and Abihu, the sons of Aaron, took their respective firepans, and after putting fire in them, placed incense on the fire and offered strange fire before the LORD, which He had not commanded them. And fire came out from the presence of the LORD and consumed them, and they died before the LORD. Then Moses said to Aaron, "It is what the LORD spoke, saying,
> 'By those who come near Me I will be treated as holy,
> And before all the people I will be honored.'"
> So Aaron, therefore, kept silent. (Lev 10:1–3)

This example employs the literal encounter with God. The result was their violation of the holiness of God, which resulted in their death.

### *The Substance*

The substance of the text is that the holiness of God is on full display. As such, irreverent worship stands in opposition to the character and nature of God and must be excised. Given the context, it is safe to say that they were offering up incense in an irreverent manner. So, the story continued, "fire came out from the presence of the LORD and consumed them, and they died before the LORD" (Lev 10:2). They did the right thing in the wrong way, and it cost them. We could speculate on their motivation, but one thing is sure: the Lord saw their act as brazen. When the Lord declared, "I will be treated as holy," we can infer that what Aaron's sons had done was just the opposite. Moses explained to Aaron that the Lord commands that he be treated as holy. In response, the text shows that Aaron remained silent. Reflecting upon this, we can see that in the midst of the Lord's discipline, it is best to stay quiet as a sign of reverence and submission to God's judgment. God will vindicate in his proper time.

### *The Structure*

The structure of the text revolves around Lev 10:1–11. There is a contrast in the text of "strange fire" and the expectation of the priests, "By those who come near Me I will be treated as holy, And before all the people I will be honored." The text's structure follows four movements. First, Nadab and Abihu offered unauthorized fire before the Lord, resulting in their immediate death by divine fire (vv. 1–2). Next, Moses explains that God's holiness must be honored by those who serve him, and Aaron remains silent in submission (v. 3). Then, the story continues, and their bodies are removed. Ultimately, the Lord forbids Aaron and his remaining sons from mourning publicly. This command from God emphasized the necessity of priestly duty over personal grief (vv. 4–7). Finally, God directs Aaron that priests must serve with sobriety, discernment, and a commitment to teaching Israel the difference between holy and common, clean and unclean (vv. 8–11). An example breakdown of the structure is as follows:

1. The sin of the fire (vv. 1–2).
2. The holiness of God (v. 3).
3. The response of mourning the judgment (vv. 4–7).
4. Clarifying Aaron's responsibility (vv. 8–11).

### *The Spirit*

The spirit of the text evokes a sense of reverence in the severity of the punishment. Ultimately, we can see that God did not tolerate the disobedience in worship. His holiness demands reverence. There was no fear of the Lord in Nadab and Abihu; there was accountability for their leadership role as priests. This encounter, although it could be categorized as negative here, revealed the leaders' disobedience. It serves as a warning call; revere the Lord, for he is holy.

### *The Summons*

The summons of the text, then, both invites and warns—it invites us to see the holiness of Christ and warns of the dire consequences that ignoring God's holiness invokes—so much so that the congregation is left with the choice to fear the Lord. For the nonbeliever, the truth stands that Nadab and Abihu tried to approach God on their own terms, bypassing his command. Sinful humanity cannot stand before God's holiness without his appointed mediator—Jesus Christ. For the believer, the Lord declared, "By those who come near Me I will be treated as holy." Therefore, those who serve God must reflect his holiness in obedience and reverence. Our holiness comes through continual submission to the cross bearing Christ's yoke. The truth universal ascribes that no matter the choice, the path forward demands a response to Christ himself.

## An Encounter Resulting in Renewal

Another text-driven example is found in Ezra's reading the scrolls in Neh 8. It stands as a paramount example from the text of the transformative power of Scripture itself. It shows how preachers can move people's hearts by proclaiming the truth, allowing the Holy Spirit to convict, and facilitating repentance and renewal. The progression of the structure begins with the gathering of the community, the clarity of Scripture read, conviction that leads to repentance and renewal, and, ultimately, transformation that leads to obedience. Ezra read from the word of God, and the conviction fell upon the people over their unholiness before a holy God. The text in focus reads,

> Ezra opened the book in the sight of all the people, for he was standing above all the people; and when he opened it, all the people stood up. Then Ezra blessed the LORD, the great God. And all the people answered, "Amen, Amen!" with the raising of their hands; then they kneeled down and worshiped the LORD with their faces to the ground. . . . Then Nehemiah, who was the governor, and Ezra the priest and scribe, and the Levites who taught the people said to all the people, "This day is holy to the LORD your God; do not mourn or weep." For all the people were weeping when they heard the words of the Law. (Neh 8:5–6, 9)

This example employs the encounter with God through the revelation of his holiness through his word. Ezra demonstrated reverence for God's word. In reading from the scroll, the transformative power of the Lord fell upon Israel so that they all wept.

### *The Substance*

The substance of the text is that preaching Scripture naturally illuminates the glory of God, which places the hearer in a position of humility and worship. Conviction against sin as well as an abiding resolve toward godliness results from the summons of the text. This transformative power of the reading of the word must be the work of the Lord. Therefore, deep dependence upon the Holy Spirit is essential for the preacher.

### The Structure

The structure of the text extends throughout the narrative of Neh 8:1–18. The text's structure can be seen in four movements. First, the structure begins with the gathering of the Israelites to hear the reading of the law (vv. 1–2). Next, the reading of the law takes precedence (vv. 3–8). This reading of the law produces a deep conviction in the hearts of the people so that they repent and are renewed in their worship of God (vv. 9–12). Finally, they renew their obedience to God through celebration of the Feast of Booths (vv. 13–18). An example breakdown of the structure is as follows:

1. The people gather in Jerusalem (vv. 1–2).
2. Ezra reads the law (vv. 3–8).
3. Repentance and renewal of the people (vv. 9–12).
4. Rediscovery of the Feast of Booths (vv. 13–18).

### The Spirit

The spirit of the text is found in the reverence in Ezra's reading from the scroll. This reverence set in motion a trajectory that changed Israel first through conviction. As the assembly gathered, Ezra read, and the weight of the holiness of God pierced the hearts of the people. The effect was not merely informational recitation of the law; it was transformational. An encounter with the living God led to weeping, repentance, and ultimately rejoicing. The word of God confronted them with the holiness of God, and the result was renewal. We, like Israel, must be careful not to allow apathy to replace genuine worship. Let us not allow complacency to rule the day but rather seek to enable the summons of the text to renew our congregations and us.

### The Summons

The summons of the text in this passage is to encounter God. The text-driven summons is essential because it requires a decision about God.[3] That encounter should call us to renewal through our justification and

3. Daniel L. Akin, "Applying a Text-Driven Sermon," in Akin et al., *Text-Driven Preaching*, 275.

sanctification. Genuine encounters through Scripture should move us from hearing to comprehension. This renewal fosters a sensitivity to the Holy Spirit. Although emotion stems from encounters with the word of the Lord, it is the outworking of living in obedience that affirms the inworking of the Holy Spirit on the heart. The consistent faithful preaching of the text results in corporate renewal. The summons brings into clear focus the person and work of Christ. This clarity about Christ compels us to choose: salvation through justification in submission to Christ or sanctification through conforming to Christ.

For the nonbeliever, the truth of the law reveals the sin that has tarnished the hearts of all mankind. Nonetheless, God does not leave his people in despair. He graciously provides forgiveness and joy through Christ's sacrifice. For the believer, the word of God continually reveals the holiness of God in contrast to our desperate state in need of God's grace. Sanctification involves not just hearing but understanding and applying God's word. Therefore, the faithful preaching of the summons of the text demands a response to the universal, revealed truth of Christ in its meaning.

## An Encounter Revealing Man's Heart

The story of Ananias and Sapphira (husband and wife) in Acts 5 stands as a peculiar narrative in the Acts of the Apostles. Grant Osborne noted, "Their names should have led them in a far different direction, for Ananias means 'Yahweh is gracious,' and Sapphira means 'beautiful.'"[4] However, they do not act in concert with their names. The text reads,

> But a man named Ananias, with his wife Sapphira, sold a piece of property, and kept back some of the price for himself, with his wife's full knowledge, and bringing a portion of it, he laid it at the apostles' feet. But Peter said, "Ananias, why has Satan filled your heart to lie to the Holy Spirit and to keep back some of the price of the land? While it remained unsold, did it not remain your own? And after it was sold, was it not under your control? Why is it that you have conceived this deed in your heart? You have not lied to men but to God." And as he heard these words, Ananias fell down and breathed his last. . . . And Peter responded to her [Sapphira], "Tell me whether you sold the land for such and such a price?" And she said, "Yes, that was the price." Then Peter said to her, "Why is it that you have agreed together to put the Spirit of the Lord to the

4. Osborne, *Acts*, 98.

> test? Behold, the feet of those who have buried your husband are at the door, and they will carry you out as well." And immediately she fell at his feet and breathed her last. (Acts 5:1–5, 8–10)

This example employs the encounter with God through the revelation of his holiness through the gospel and the power of the Holy Spirit. The result was the judgment of death.

### *The Substance*

The substance of the text is that God is omniscient and that the community of Christ must be marked by holy fear and integrity. Ananias and Sapphira lied to the Holy Spirit, and the consequences were dire. It was not about the money; it was about the heart and the attitude toward God that was behind the scheming. The nature of their sin rested in their attempt to gain honor without true sacrifice. There is a long laundry list of attributes that could be ascribed to them. They were spiritual frauds, praise seekers, hypocrites, and the list goes on. Nevertheless, the one thing Peter declared was, "Why has Satan filled your heart?" He identified them as adversaries of God. God is holy; therefore, their actions were seen in the opposite light. Peter then corrects them with a series of questions striking to the heart of their selfish motivation. These questions are their indictment, leading to their judgment by the Holy Spirit.

### *The Structure*

The structure of the text spans Acts 5:1–11. The specific encounter is highlighted to establish the call to respond within the text. The structure unfolds in three movements. First, Ananias and Sapphira conspired to deceive the church by presenting a partial gift as if it were the whole (vv. 1–2). Then Peter confronts each of them separately, exposing their lie as an offense against the Holy Spirit, and both fall dead under God's judgment (vv. 3–10). Finally, the narrative closes with the community's response, as great fear seizes the whole church and all who hear of these events, underscoring the seriousness of integrity before God (v. 11). An example breakdown of the structure is as follows:

1. The deception plot is laid out (vv. 1–2).

2. The exposure and corresponding judgment (vv. 3–10).
3. The response of the church (v. 11).

### *The Spirit*

The spirit of the text is found in the suddenness of God's judgment. The weight of this difficulty must not escape us as we preach. The sudden nature of their deaths connects closely with that of Nadab and Abihu (as previously discussed). The holiness of God demands a harsh punishment for violation of God's character. There is great difficulty in preaching this passage, given the nature of the gospel. Nevertheless, Osborne astutely noted, "There is great reward for those who are faithful (Barnabas) and great punishment for those who are not (Ananias and Sapphira). He expects his people to surrender all to him and follow the guidance of the Spirit. Being a Christian is not a halfway thing. He demands our all."[5]

### *The Summons*

The summons of the text is that God is omniscient and not to be lied to. The proper fear of the Lord would have prevented such a catastrophe. This passage calls to mind the holiness of God and our need to be holy, just as he is holy. In response to the revelation of God through the text, we must see the holiness of God in stark contrast to the world's clamoring for position and power. Essentially, this truth should call us to take God's promises seriously. For the nonbeliever, the fact that God holds life in his hands should commend an urgency to respond to God, as no one is guaranteed tomorrow. For the believer, the summons should compel us to vividly recognize our responsibility to obey the Lord in every aspect of our lives.

## An Encounter Revealing Man's Motivation

Let us take a moment to examine the story of Simon the magician found in Acts 8:9–24. The context shows that Simon was enamored with the power of the Holy Spirit, seeing the apostles imparting the Spirit through the laying on of hands. The focus of our text reads,

5. Osborne, *Acts*, 102.

> Now, when Simon saw that the Spirit was bestowed through the laying on of the apostles' hands, he offered them money, saying, "Give this authority to me as well, so that everyone on whom I lay my hands may receive the Holy Spirit." But Peter said to him, "May your silver perish with you, because you thought you could obtain the gift of God with money! You have no part or portion in this matter, for your heart is not right before God. Therefore, repent of this wickedness of yours, and pray the Lord that, if possible, the intention of your heart may be forgiven you. For I see that you are in the gall of bitterness and in the bondage of iniquity." But Simon answered and said, "Pray to the Lord for me yourselves, so that nothing of what you have said may come upon me." (Acts 8:18–24)

This example employs the encounter with God through the revelation of his holiness through the gospel and the power of the Holy Spirit. The result was the rebuke of the apostles and the call for renewed repentance.

### *The Substance*

The substance of the text is as follows: the apostolic confirmation of the gospel message to the Samaritans despite Simon's impure motivations. We can see that Simon's motivation was to control this power. He had the wrong motivation.

### *The Structure*

The structure of the text flows from the narrative found in Acts 8:9–24. The text's structure unfolds in three movements. First, Simon the magician's reputation and influence among the Samaritans are contrasted with the genuine conversions that follow Philip's preaching (vv. 9–13). Then, the apostles arrive to confirm the new believers, and Simon, corruptly, seeks to purchase spiritual authority, exposing his misguided motives (vv. 14–19). Finally, Peter rebukes Simon, calling him to repentance, and the episode closes with Simon's plea for mercy, highlighting the seriousness of integrity in the Spirit's work (vv. 20–24). The example structure of the text is as follows:

1. Simon's reputation and the power of the gospel (vv. 9–13).
2. Simon's motivation is revealed in light of the power of the Holy Spirit (vv. 14–19).
3. Peter's rebuke and call for repentance (vv. 20–24).

### *The Spirit*

The spirit of the text stands as a hopeful confidence in the propagation and protection of the gospel through the power of the Holy Spirit. Despite Simon's selfish motivations, Peter and John's presence validates that Samaritans truly belong to the same Spirit-filled community, underscoring unity across boundaries. Osborne wrote, "He thought God and the Spirit could be bought from the leaders of the church, and then he would control God and once more be 'the Great Power of God.'"[6] Just a little reading in the greater context reveals Simon's history with magic in Samaria. Moreover, the request he posed, "Give this authority to me as well, so that everyone on whom I lay my hands may receive the Holy Spirit" (v. 19), is very telling of his motivation. It was not for worship of God that he desired this power, but for notoriety and personal gain. What he received in response was not the blessing of the Holy Spirit but a stark rebuke and warning over his eternal soul. Peter sternly declared, "May your silver perish with you, because you thought you could obtain the gift of God with money. . . . Repent of this wickedness of yours" (vv. 20, 22). His heart was laid bare to the apostles, and Peter saw through the charade.

### *The Summons*

The summons of the text shows us the danger of separating God's freely given grace from the sanctification that reorients our hearts toward God. Salvation without sanctification leads to distorted motives, while sanctification without justification becomes empty moralism. Together, they reveal that grace saves us and then transforms us. Unlike the previous example of Ananias and Sapphira, Simon was rebuked and offered a second chance at repentance. For the nonbeliever, salvation and the infilling of the Holy Spirit are gifts of God's grace alone and not commodities to be earned or

6. Osborne, *Acts*, 162.

purchased. True salvation requires a heart transformed by Christ through genuine repentance and faith. It is not sufficient to ascribe to rites and rituals as an outward sign of assent. For the believer, God's holiness confronts ambition, pride, and self-serving desires. How we respond to the Spirit's correction reveals our submission to Christ. Holiness reorients us from self-glory to God's glory.

## An Encounter Resulting in Commission

I hope we are all familiar with the story of Paul's conversion in Acts 9. Paul (also known as Saul) set out to destroy the church, yet God had other plans. God's divine revelation of himself on the road to Damascus turned into a paradigm shift for Paul. The text reads,

> As he was traveling, it happened that he was approaching Damascus, and suddenly a light from heaven flashed around him; and he fell to the ground and heard a voice saying to him, "Saul, Saul, why are you persecuting Me?" And he said, "Who are You, Lord?" And He said, "I am Jesus whom you are persecuting, but get up and enter the city, and it will be told you what you must do." . . . Now there was a disciple at Damascus named Ananias; and the Lord said to him in a vision, "Ananias." And he said, "Here I am, Lord." And the Lord said to him, "Get up and go to the street called Straight, and inquire at the house of Judas for a man from Tarsus named Saul, for he is praying." (Acts 9:3–6, 10–11)

This example employs the literal encounter with God through the risen Lord Jesus. The result of this encounter was Saul's commission to the gentiles, further fulfilling Acts 1:8.

### *The Substance*

The substance of the text reveals that an encounter with the living Christ results in transformation and a call to live for something greater than self. In addition, this is a significant shift in the commission of the gospel toward the gentiles; thus, further fulfilling Acts 1:8. This encounter with God called upon Paul to make a decision: acknowledge the lordship of Christ or continue attacking Christ himself. It was no accident that Jesus declared, "Saul, Saul, why are you persecuting Me?" (Acts 9:4). An attack against the church was an attack on Christ himself. Christ revealed himself to Paul to transform him. Paul went from persecutor to proselyte, from blasphemer to worshiper, from accuser to advocate, and from opposer to advocate. His identity transformed from "Jew of Jews" to "bondservant of Christ." This was a demonstration of the power of the Holy Spirit at work in the life of someone who encountered the word.

### *The Structure*

The structure of the text stands around Acts 9:1–19. The text's structure can be seen in four movements. First, we can see the hate and hostility of Saul seeking to arrest Christians (vv. 1–2). Next, there is an encounter with Christ that leaves him blind and helpless (vv. 3–9). Then, the story reveals the reluctant Ananias as the mediator for Saul (vv. 10–15). Finally, Saul is commissioned to take the gospel to the gentiles (vv. 16–19). This all speaks to the transformative power of the risen Lord Jesus. An example breakdown of the structure is as follows:

1. The hostile nature of Saul (vv. 1–2).
2. The encounter with Christ (vv. 3–9).
3. The reluctant mediator (vv. 10–15).
4. Saul's commission to the gentiles (vv. 16–19).

### *The Spirit*

The spirit of the text shows the weight of Paul's encounter with the living Christ. This encounter forever changes the trajectory of his life. He was now commissioned for the sake of the gospel. In the same fashion, we should, through the summons of the text, have our lives changed. Like Paul, we must caution ourselves, our congregation, and even our own hearts, against the dangers of apathetic faith. James Stewart clearly attested, "The indispensable centre of Christianity is Christ; and we ruin our religion if we centre it anywhere else."[7]

7. Stewart, *Faith to Proclaim*, 143.

### *The Summons*

The summons of the text should pull into clear focus the person and work of Christ. The congregation is left with the choice of their commission: justification by Christ or sanctification through Christ. For the nonbeliever, Saul was actively opposing Christ, yet God intervened. God's grace reaches even the worst sinner. This truth underscores the gospel truth that salvation is not earned but received through the person and work of Christ. For the believer, sanctification means God not only saves us but repurposes our lives for his mission. The necessity of daily surrender begins with humility before the Lord, recognizing our dependence on the gospel of Jesus Christ.

## Conclusion

Preaching a sermon without calling upon the audience to respond to the summons is as fruitless as baking bread without yeast or trying to drive a car without gas. Daniel Akin wrote, "Faithful expositors are not only responsible to explain and expound the meaning of the text; they are also responsible to apply the text, preaching for a life-changing verdict from the audience."[8] The summons stands as the core of the encounter with God. It bridges the sermon to the universal truth of the person and work of Christ. The summons for salvation commands repentance of sin and faith in Christ. Nothing else matters to the person who sashays down the wide path toward hell. Correct behavior does not save; only Christ can and does save those who repent and believe. But for those who profess faith in Christ, the summons of the text leads us to godliness in Christ. Greg Gilbert wrote, "Realize that the fruit you bear is merely that—the fruit of a tree already made good by God's grace in Christ. To rely on your own Christian fruit to secure God's favor is ultimately to shift your faith from Jesus to yourself. And that is no salvation at all."[9]

8. Daniel L. Akin, "Applying a Text-Driven Sermon," in Akin et al., *Text-Driven Preaching*, 281.

9. Gilbert, *What Is the Gospel?*, 83.

# Conclusion

I argue that text-driven preaching stands as an exemplary model for expository preaching. The aspect of taking a text, explaining it from its substance, structure, and spirit, and then applying it to the modern audience from those timeless truths provides Holy Spirit–backed power in the pulpit. In addition, the summons of the text merely reinforces an already exceptional preaching model, illuminating the bridge between the "whatness" that the text calls for us to respond to and the "howness" of application that contextualizes that command. Having established the ubiquity of Christ throughout Scripture, we can boldly attest that the gospel is at the heart of every text of Scripture.

## A Text-Driven View of the Summons

The text-driven preaching model aims to stay in lockstep with the text's meaning. The substance captures the meaning through exegesis, the structure illuminates it through linguistics, and the spirit expounds it by capturing the feel of the text. Moreover, Steven Smith addressed concerns regarding 2 Tim 4:2 as the natural crux for preachers to defend text-driven preaching. Instead, he contends, "The reason text-driven preaching is so compelling does not come from one single verse."[1] His argument rests upon the whole of Scripture and the pastor's responsibility to "explain scripture" to their people.[2] He rightly asserts that text-driven preaching goes beyond mere stylistic homiletics. Text-driven preaching is a deep-seated conviction that is a theologically driven preaching philosophy.[3] Furthermore, illustrat-

1. Smith, *Recapturing the Voice of God*, 22.
2. Smith, *Recapturing the Voice of God*, 23.
3. Smith, *Recapturing the Voice of God*, 24.

ing Smith's theological conviction, he writes, "This work is offered for a generation that will surrender preaching so that every generation can hear God over our voices, a generation that will bear the cross in the pulpit to preach the cross from the pulpit, a generation dying to preach."[4] He rightly contends that expository, text-driven preaching is the highest form of preaching because it is rooted in and proceeds from the text.

However, as it pertains to biblical exhortation, Smith contends that, from the heart of every sermon, the gospel should flow and that it must be woven into every sermon; the preacher must call others to respond to Christ in faith.[5] Smith's gospel conviction is rightly rooted in a Christ-centered hermeneutic. His application, exhortation, and appeal demonstrate a resolve to connect to the gospel. He defines exhortation as "the application of the text to the listeners that impresses them to act on the text."[6] He further delves into the riches of church history by examining the role of exhortation. He surmises that the application reveals how the hearer must respond to the text, whereas the exhortation illuminates why they do so.[7] The application informs what the text says to do, and the summons reveals why the hearer must do it.

## The Implication of the Summons Considering 2 Timothy 4:1–5

The notion of expository preaching holds its footing in the annals of history. From Origen and Chrysostom to W. A. Criswell and Steven Smith, commitment to expository preaching is rooted in taking a text, explaining it, and applying it.[8] Faithfulness to the text of Scripture is the aim of every text-driven expositor. The preacher must speak when Scripture speaks and remain silent when the text is silent. However, this research shows that Paul's commendation of Timothy to preach the word anchors in the necessity of reproof, rebuke, and exhortation. Each of those verbs demands a decision that rests at the feet of the hearer in response to the gospel. Although not explicitly stated, preaching for a response is implicit in Paul's chosen verbs. To reprove serves to convince, to rebuke reveals the hearers' need in

4. Smith, *Dying to Preach*, 175.
5. Smith, *Recapturing the Voice of God*, 98.
6. Gallaty and Smith, *Preaching*, 119.
7. Gallaty and Smith, *Preaching*, 121.
8. Walker, *Let the Text Talk*, 134.

their dire state, and to exhort is to urge the hearer back to the gospel. Each of these verbs calls the hearer to change their mind and—in the case of exhortation—to turn back.

Paul commands Timothy to exhort in connection with preaching the word. Implicit is the idea that the summons is simply the truth in the text to which a person must respond. The summons re-presents the call to physical action, to adjust a view of God, or to both. Fundamentally, Scripture is the revelation of God to mankind. The implications of each passage in context call for deeper worship of God through the revelation of himself. This understanding implies a perspicuity of meaning from each text—a deeper faith in God. That deeper faith connects to a relationship with Jesus Christ.

Moreover, the summons within the text is the truth that the author of the text is commending to his hearers. The whole of Scripture is the divine revelation of who God is and what he has done. From that understanding, the summons of the text commands the reader to respond—either walking in obedience or transforming how they see God. Therefore, the summons of the text naturally draws from the redemptive nature of the cross. The gospel must be present in the expositor's mind as they exegete the text. Bryan Chapell contends, "Accurate expositors use a magnifying glass and a fish-eye lens, knowing that a magnifying glass can unravel mysteries in a raindrop but fail to expose a storm gathering on the horizon."[9] Ultimately, the power of the gospel must infiltrate the innermost affections of the heart, permeate the soul, and compel the hearer to respond.[10] The summons must align with a more excellent canonical view to ensure biblical consistency with the whole of Scripture. Therefore, the conviction of the centrality of the gospel in preaching must be unmistakable. Paul commends preaching the word—the message of Christ as argued—and in preaching, the word must reprove, rebuke, and exhort.

## The Biblical and Theological Implications

Biblical and theological implications of the summons rest firmly in the reproof, rebuke, and exhortation. This summons appears in both explicit and implicit forms, depending on the text's intended meaning. Within its explicit form, Scripture reveals the person and work of Christ. Prayer and

9. See Bryan Chapell, "Redemptive-Historic View," in Gibson and Kim, *Homiletics and Hermeneutics*, 5.

10. Calvin, *Christian Life*, 13–14.

reflection upon the text illuminate the biblical and theological connection to the person and work of Christ. The text should expound the very heart of Scripture—God's divine revelation of himself to his creation. Kenneth Langley posited, "Authoritative, God-glorifying preaching depends on fidelity to the text . . . grounding the message in the words of Scripture, showing listeners where the assertions of the sermon come from in the passage exposited."[11] The argument of the sermon must be anchored to the propositions within Scripture. Josh Smith concurred, "If text-driven preaching allows the text to drive every aspect of the sermon when the text speaks to the will and calls for change, the sermon must do the same."[12] However, the intent of the text is "for teaching, for reproof, for correction, for training in righteousness" (2 Tim 3:16). Paul Tripp wrote, "The only hope for our story is that we would be part of His story of redemption. The only way to approach the events of our lives is to approach them redemptively."[13] The training in righteousness declared by the apostle Paul catalyzes one's participation in God's redemptive story. Thus, it is crucial to notice that the pericope of the text should culminate in a call of God's word for the hearer to respond. John Piper asserted, "[The preacher] must pray and preach so that a new mental framework is created for seeing the world. Ultimately, this is not [his] doing. God must do it."[14] God's word compels the response of changing one's thoughts about him or walking in closer obedience to his commands.

## The Philosophical Value

The philosophical value of the summons is in gaining a convictional, holistic view of the text. The summons of the text naturally draws toward the redemptive nature of the cross. Therefore, the philosophical perspective must be present in the expositor's mind with the cross in mind. Bryan Chapell contended, "Accurate expositors use both a magnifying glass and a fish-eye lens, knowing that a magnifying glass can unravel mysteries in a raindrop but can fail to expose a storm gathering on the horizon."[15] The

11. See Kenneth Langley, "Theocentric View," in Gibson and Kim, *Homiletics and Hermeneutics*, 95.

12. Smith, *Preaching for a Verdict*, 37.

13. Tripp, *War of Words*, 162.

14. Piper, *Supremacy of God*, 128.

15. See Bryan Chapell, "Redemptive-Historic View," in Gibson and Kim, *Homiletics*

summons must align with a grander redemptive view to ensure consistency with Scripture. This redemption compels the hearer to respond to God's redemptive plan—confirmed through the person and work of Christ. Smith articulated, "If God's word always demands a response (as Jas 1:22 indicates), and the sermon is a faithful declaration of the Word of God, the sermon should call for a response. An exhortation is embedded in every text."[16] The call to redemption rests in the revelation of Christ throughout, summoning the hearer to embrace the truth propositions about the person of Christ, his work, and his kingdom.

Moreover, we must not neglect the philosophical view of the text, which speaks first to the preacher. Charles Spurgeon wrote, "[God] will work in a place where a warmhearted man is preaching to men the truth that he has himself received, all the while earnestly desiring their salvation, and ready to guide them further in the ways of the Lord as soon as they are saved."[17] Spurgeon's conviction was that the text first ministers to the preacher and that the preacher—from internal conviction—sets forth before himself the intentional work of preparing the way of salvation through preaching the word. As A. G. Sertillanges asserted, "Before giving out the truth, acquire it for yourself, and do not waste the seed of your sowing."[18] In preaching, the word of God must first take hold of the preacher.

In addition, Hershael York and Bert Decker expounded upon this conviction when they asserted, "We [do not] just want them to know the truth; we want them to do the truth. Our conclusion, therefore, should reflect that commitment."[19] It is insufficient to provide head knowledge without compelling the response toward greater godliness from the hearer. Abraham Kuruvilla referred to this approach as Pericopal theology. He wrote, "[This approach seeks to] go only as high as one needs to, staying as low as one can. All of these transactions [substantiating conclusions with exegesis] are in aid of one ultimate goal: to arrive at an application that is valid."[20] Therefore, it is paramount that the summons of the text must first compel the preacher to respond.

---

*and Hermeneutics*, 5.

16. Smith, *Preaching for a Verdict*, 95.

17. Spurgeon, *Soul Winner*, 45.

18. Sertillanges, *Intellectual Life*, 13.

19. York and Decker, *Preaching with Bold Assurance*, 188.

20. Kuruvilla, *Privilege the Text*, 135.

## The Pedagogical Need

The pedagogical needs of the summons rest upon teaching preachers to compel their congregants to look to Christ as the focus of faith and hope for the world. The summons transforms the sermon from a passive experience to an active engagement. The faithful proclamation of the summons acknowledges the need for listeners to act. From the summons, the preacher can connect to the application. Several methods exist to discover the truth of Christ, as revealed in Scripture. For example, David Helm stated that there are "four categories of connections that I think will help you engage in biblical-theological reflection: prophetic fulfillment, historical trajectory, themes, and analogies."[21] Tony Merida espoused that preachers must wrestle with "contending and contextualizing" and that too much emphasis on the former leads to "irrelevancy" while the latter results in "syncretism."[22] Further, Bryan Chapell argued, "If the application loses sight of the Fallen Condition Focus, the message will degenerate into a handful of legalisms tacked onto randomly selected observations."[23] Also, Paul Scott Wilson posited that there are "four basic grammatical elements of the sermon, or Pages. . . . Page One is the trouble in the biblical text. . . . Page Two is the trouble in our world. . . . Page Three is grace in the biblical text. . . . Page Four is grace in our world."[24] While more methods for establishing the Christ connection within the text exist, the summons must stand anchored to the meaning, and from that meaning, the call to respond must flow.

In addition, the preacher must learn how to present a summons to move the congregation toward action in a gentle manner. The book of Proverbs reveals that "a gentle answer turns away wrath, but a harsh word stirs up anger" (15:1). Therefore, the preacher's most significant movement toward the congregation is toward love and affection for the gospel. Preachers must learn to allow the reproof, rebuke, and exhortation within the text to drive the summons to the hearers. Sertillanges asserted that "every truth is life" and that truth is "a way leading to the end of man."[25] Therefore,

21. Helm, *Expositional Preaching*, 114.

22. Merida, *Faithful Preaching*, 198.

23. Chapell, *Christ-Centered Preaching*, 212.

24. See Paul Scott Wilson, "Law-Gospel View," in Gibson and Kim, *Homiletics and Hermeneutics*, 132–33.

25. Sertillanges, *Intellectual Life*, 13.

preachers must learn that the summons must speak and instruct the hearer to draw near to God in salvation through justification and sanctification.

## The Practical Application

The summons of the text provides practical application for preaching. Text-driven preaching develops the text and draws its natural conclusion in the summons of the text, which rests upon the gospel connection. The most significant spiritual need of the nonbeliever is the gospel of Jesus. Likewise, an equally valid concept is that the believer's most significant spiritual need is the gospel of Jesus. Therefore, the text's summons results in a twofold outcome—it commands believers toward holiness and compels nonbelievers toward repentance and faith in Jesus Christ.

Consequently, faithfulness to the text demands that every text-driven sermon hold a summons within its structure. The culmination of the text-driven sermon must call the believer to deeper faith and obedience and the unbeliever to repentance and faith in Jesus as both Savior and Lord. B. H. Carroll said it best in his message "An Address on Evangelism" when he declared, "Brethren, give me evangelists. Deny not fins to things that must swim against the tide, nor wings to things that must fly against the wind."[26] The implication of Carroll's request rings true today in applying the summons within the substance-structure-spirit framework of the text-driven preaching model. Eloquence alone is insufficient to sway the hearts of the congregation. Instead, spiritual persuasion demands dependence upon the sufficiency of the word and the power of the Holy Spirit.

## Salvation as a Product of the Summons

The primacy of the summons directs the unbeliever toward salvation. The essence of this assertion rests on the necessity of the heart's transformation through the gospel before the sanctifying work of the Holy Spirit in the believer's life. The Holy Spirit kindles faith before the works follow suit. The summons of the text, then, holds a salvific component. Hershael York and Bert Decker asserted that the goal of the sermon should be to produce practical application.[27] William Arnold declared,

26. From "An Address on Evangelism," in Carroll, *B. H. Carroll Pulpit*, 167.

27. York and Decker, *Preaching with Bold Assurance*, 11.

> The objective basis and means of salvation are God's sovereign and gracious choice to be "God with us" in the person of Jesus Christ, described as both author and mediator of salvation (Heb. 2:10; 7:25). But the movement of Jesus' life goes through the cross and resurrection. It is, therefore, "Christ crucified" that is of central importance for salvation (1 Cor. 1:23), for "Christ died for our sins according to the Scriptures" (1 Cor. 15:3) and was handed over to death for our trespasses (Rom. 4:25).[28]

The central focus of salvation is the demonstration of God's love for mankind through the sacrificial act of Christ. The means of salvation rest entirely upon the work of Christ. Therefore, the saving aspect of the summons anchors the text to the person and work of Jesus. For the unbeliever, the implication of the gospel is to repent and respond to the gospel message as recorded in the book of Acts (2:38, 3:19, 26:20). This salvation connotes the past, present, and future work of Christ within the dimensions of sanctification culminating in glorification.

Repentance becomes a central theme, representing a fundamental aspect of the relationship between humanity and God. It changes the mind, turns people away from sin, and returns them to God. Repentance characterizes a sincere change of heart and mind, followed closely by the person's outward volition to walk according to God's command and allow God to set them apart.

We must not conflate the text's call to respond with a call to "walk down an aisle." Instead, each text of Scripture illuminates the person and/or work of Christ in some fashion. We must respond to that revelation. The preacher should strive to capture what the text sets for the hearer "to know, do, and believe" in the sermon.[29] The saving application of the summons is in response to Christ's revelation within the text's central idea, which is to turn to Christ in repentance and faith. O. S. Hawkins and Matt Queen asserted,

> Gospel invitations should be offered in public settings because of: (1) the New Testament's precedent of publicly issuing gospel invitations in order to make disciples; (2) unbeliever's lack of familiarity in knowing how to respond to gospel invitations when they are convicted of their sins by the Holy Spirit; (3) the implicit nature of preaching and its relationship to gospel invitations; and (4) the

28. See William Arnold, "Salvation," in Elwell, *Evangelical Dictionary*, 702.

29. Rogers, *Preaching for Impact*, 76.

> historical record of how preachers have issued gospel invitations that God has used to bring people to faith in Christ.[30]

The implicit nature of the saving work of the gospel message nestled within the word of God demands attention. The hope of Christ—as revealed in Scripture—poses a challenge to the hearer to embrace or reject. The gospel proclaims God's glorification through his work of grace, demonstrated in the person and mission of Christ, offering humanity reconciliation and peace with him. Therefore, the call of the gospel must permeate the whole person—mind, emotions, and will—to the necessity of salvation through Christ.

## Sanctification as a Product of the Summons

The summons of the text for those who already believe in Christ points to greater sanctification. The preacher must recognize the summons of the text toward greater obedience to the call of God to be set apart. The summons to obey exists throughout Scripture. Within the Old Testament, God spoke to Israel, instructing them to "be careful to do" (Deut 8:1) all that he had commanded, culminating in the declaration, "Do not forget the LORD your God" (Deut 8:11). This passage sets the stage for the call to obedience. The prophets exhorted Israel to obedience. Samuel succinctly stated, "To obey is better than a sacrifice," setting obedience as the greater goal (1 Sam 15:22). Finally, the leaders demonstrated the call to faithful obedience. Joshua declared, "Be careful to do according to all the law which Moses My servant commanded you," exemplifying the benefit of sanctification (Josh 1:7). The culmination of obedience drives believers toward further Christlikeness. Christ set the example that believers must follow. Bradford Mullen asserted, "Christ was qualified to sanctify because he himself had been sanctified through suffering (Heb. 2:10–11). First, Jesus Christ was the only human being since the fall to live a continuously, perfectly sanctified life. . . . Second, he was vocationally sanctified. Christ did what the Father called him to do (John 5:19, 30, 36; 6:38; 8:28–29; 12:49)."[31]

Additionally, the New Testament demonstrates the continued necessity of sanctification through the summons. Jesus called his hearers to respond to his teaching by saying, "The one who has two tunics is to share

30. Hawkins and Queen, *Gospel Invitation*, 27.

31. See Bradford A. Mullen, "Sanctification," in Elwell, *Evangelical Dictionary*, 710.

with him who has none; and he who has food is to do likewise" (Luke 3:11). Here, Jesus' command was not to salvation but obedience to God. Additionally, Jesus declared that to love him meant to keep his commandments (John 14:15). However, the gospel call is not merely limited to the believer's obedience. Furthermore, in the first century, believers followed Christ by declaring the hope of the gospel. Peter compelled his hearers to "repent, and . . . be baptized" (Acts 2:38). Paul compelled his hearers to pursue holiness. He declared, "Shall we sin because we are not under law but under grace? May it never be" (Rom 6:15). Of Paul's writing to the churches, James Thompson wrote, "Although Paul insists that he does not 'persuade people' (Gal 1:10), his task in Galatians, as in other letters, is to persuade the readers to take the right course of action."[32] James drew attention to the connection between faith and work (Jas 2:17).

It is expected that believers will respond to the person and work of Christ. York and Decker asserted, "The proposition arises from the text, which is why we say it must be discovered from the main theme and thrust of the passage."[33] The sanctifying application then anchors to the truth proposition about Christ uncovered in the text through exegesis. The sermon's application for sanctification drives the hearer's practical need, as revealed in the text. The summons of the text calls to the hearer and divinely meets them in their spiritual need toward sanctification. The summons results in sanctification revealed in the text through Christ's nature and character, and the Holy Spirit compels the mind, heart, and will toward becoming more holy and Christlike.

## Conclusion

Shifting cultural convictions, evolving ecclesiastical methodologies, and a decline in moral standards underscore the necessity of faithfulness in the proclamation of Scripture. Preaching remains central to the life and mission of the church. Where the preaching ministry goes, the church will follow; the weight of that responsibility is enormous, and preachers across the world should feel it acutely. Let us seek to include the summons of the text and extend the current text-driven preaching model. Let us strive toward textual faithfulness as we submit to the text and re-present the life-changing word of God to those within our pastoral care. Since text-driven preaching

32. Thompson, *Apostle of Persuasion*, 169.

33. York and Decker, *Preaching with Bold Assurance*, 139.

seeks, as its chief aim, the truth that God has spoken, let us commit to preaching the word. God has spoken through his written word; let us strive to base our preaching on it, anchored in the text.

# APPENDIX

# Text-Driven Preaching Worksheet

## Reflections on the Substance of the Text

1) What is the immediate context of the passage (the preceding and following verses)?

______________________________________________

______________________________________________

______________________________________________

______________________________________________

2) What is the main idea or central thought that the author is communicating?

______________________________________________

______________________________________________

______________________________________________

______________________________________________

3) What events or circumstances surround the writer and his original audience? What cultural references exist in the passage?

______________________________________________

______________________________________________

______________________________________________

______________________________________________

4) What theological references exist in the passage? What keywords, terms, or concepts are repeated?

5) What is the author's main aim for his audience? Summarize this thought in one sentence.

6) What theological truth does this passage reveal that holds universal application?

## Reflections on the Structure of the Text

1) How has the author organized this passage? How does the passage naturally break into movements, scenes, or arguments?

2) What grammatical markers exist to demonstrate the shape/flow of the text? Identify the indicatives, imperatives, independent clauses, dependent clauses, conjoiners, comparison/contrasts, etc.

3) What is the logical progression of the text (cause to effect, problem to solution, truth to response, etc.)?

4) What is the relationship of the passage to the larger argument (supporting, explaining, illustrating, etc.)?

5) What structural elements must be preserved in the sermon to maintain textual integrity?

6) What key terms appear in the passage?

## Reflections on the Spirit of the Text

1) What genre of literature is the passage?

2) What was the author's intended emotional tone within the text (lament, comfort, rejoicing, warning, judgment, etc.)?

_________________________________________________________________

_________________________________________________________________

_________________________________________________________________

_________________________________________________________________

3) How do the substance and structure inform the tone of the text (pastoral, theological, biblical, etc.)?

_________________________________________________________________

_________________________________________________________________

_________________________________________________________________

_________________________________________________________________

4) What vital doctrinal truths reveal the tone and weight of importance within the text?

_________________________________________________________________

_________________________________________________________________

_________________________________________________________________

_________________________________________________________________

5) What is the universal truth revealed within the spirit of the text?

_________________________________________________________________

_________________________________________________________________

_________________________________________________________________

_________________________________________________________________

6) What would be lost if the tone of the sermon did not match the tone of the text?

_________________________________________________________________

_________________________________________________________________

_________________________________________________________________

_________________________________________________________________

## Reflections on the Summons of the Text

1) What does the passage reveal about God the Father, God the Son, or God the Holy Spirit?

2) Does the passage explicitly or implicitly connect to the gospel? Which aspect of the gospel connection exists (i.e., the person and work of Christ)?

3) What specific actions, attitudes, or commitments are directly connected to the text? Does the text illuminate the character and nature of God (indicative) or explicitly call for a response (imperative)?

4) How does the gospel reinforce the main idea of the text? Where does the main idea of the text point to the gospel? (See *The Gospel Method*, figure 8.1 in chapter 8.)

5) What specific response does the text call for (faith, repentance, obedience, worship, etc.)?

______________________________________________

______________________________________________

______________________________________________

______________________________________________

6) How can modern hearers respond to the text in faith? What is the sanctifying truth? What is the justifying truth?

______________________________________________

______________________________________________

______________________________________________

______________________________________________

# Bibliography


Adam, Peter. *Speaking God's Words: A Practical Theology of Preaching*. Vancouver: Regent College, 2004.

Akin, Daniel L., et al., eds. *Text-Driven Preaching: God's Word at the Heart of Every Sermon*. Nashville: B&H Academic, 2010.

Allen, Roland. *Missionary Methods, St. Paul's or Ours: A Study of the Church in the Four Provinces*. London: Pantanos Classics, 1912.

Aristotle. *On Rhetoric: A Theory of Civil Discourse*. Translated by George A. Kennedy. London: CRW, 2009.

Ashford, Bruce Riley, ed. *Theology and Practice of Mission*. Nashville: B&H Academic, 2011.

Augustine. *On Teaching Christianity: De Doctrina Christiana*. Translated by Edmund Hill. Hyde Park, NY: New City, 2002.

Baird, A. C. *Rhetoric: A Philosophical Inquiry*. New York: Ronald, 1965.

Barrett, C. K. *The Epistle to the Romans*. Rev. ed. Black's New Testament Commentary. Edited by Henry Chadwick. London: A&C, 1991.

Barth, Karl. *The Call to Discipleship*. Minneapolis: Fortress, 2003.

———. *Homiletics*. Translated by Geoffrey W. Bromiley and Donald E. Daniels. Louisville: Westminster John Knox, 1966.

Bates, Matthew W. *Salvation by Allegiance Alone: Rethinking Faith, Works, and the Gospel of Jesus the King*. Grand Rapids: Baker Academic, 2017.

Begg, Alistair. *Preaching for God's Glory*. Wheaton, IL: Crossway, 2011.

Bizzell, Patricia, and Bruce Herzberg, eds. *The Rhetorical Tradition: Readings from Classical Times to the Present*. 2nd ed. Boston: Bedford/St. Martins, 2001.

Black, David Alan. *Learn to Read New Testament Greek*. 3rd ed. Nashville: B&H, 2009.

Black, David Alan, et al., eds. *Linguistics and New Testament Interpretation: Essays on Discourse Analysis*. Nashville: Broadman, 1992.

Bock, Darrell L. *Acts*. Baker Exegetical Commentary on the New Testament. Edited by Robert W. Yarbrough and Robert H. Stein. Grand Rapids: Baker Academic, 2007.

———. *Recovering the Real Lost Gospel: Reclaiming the Gospel as Good News*. Nashville: B&H, 2010.

Bonhoeffer, Dietrich. *The Cost of Discipleship*. New York: Scribner Paper Fiction, 1963.

Bradford, Carl J. "Schooling the Gospel: An Investigation of British and German Schools of Kerygmatic Interpretation in the Twentieth and Twenty-First Centuries." PhD diss., Southwestern Baptist Theological Seminary, 2018.

Bray, Gerald. *Biblical Interpretation: Past and Present*. Downers Grove, IL: InterVarsity, 1996.

Brown, Stephen W., et al. *A Voice in the Wilderness: Clear Preaching in a Complicated World*. Sisters, OR: Multnomah, 1993.

Bruce, F. F. *1 and 2 Thessalonians*. Word Biblical Commentary 45. Edited by Bruce M. Metzger et al. Grand Rapids: Zondervan, 2015.

———. *The Book of the Acts*. Rev. ed. The New International Commentary of the New Testament. Edited by Joel B. Green. Grand Rapids: Eerdmans, 1988.

Bultmann, Rudolf K. *The Second Letter to the Corinthians*. Edited by Erich Dinkler. Minneapolis: Augsburg, 1985.

———. *Theology of the New Testament*. Vol. 1. Translated by Kendrick Grobel. New York: Scribner's Sons, 1951.

Calvin, John. *Commentaries on the Four Last Books of Moses*. Vol. 3. Translated by Charles W. Bingham. Bellingham, WA: Logos Bible Software, 2010.

———. *A Little Book on the Christian Life*. Translated by Aaron C. Delinger and Burk Parsons. Orlando: Reformed Trust, 2017.

Carroll, B. H. *The B. H. Carroll Pulpit*. Edited by Adam W. Greenway. Legacy Series. Fort Worth: Seminary Hill, 2021.

Carroll, John T. *Luke: A Commentary*. The New Testament Library. Edited by C. Clifton Black et al. Louisville: Westminster John Knox, 2012.

Carson, D. A. *Exegetical Fallacies*. 2nd ed. Grand Rapids: Baker Academic, 1996.

Carson, D. A., and Douglas J. Moo. *An Introduction to the New Testament*. 2nd ed. Grand Rapids: Zondervan Academic, 2005.

Chapell, Bryan. *Christ-Centered Preaching: Redeeming the Expository Sermon*. 2nd ed. Nashville: Baker Academic, 2005.

Charles, H. B. *On Preaching: Personal and Pastoral Insights for the Preparation and Practice of Preaching*. Chicago: Moody, 2014.

Collins, Raymond F. *1 & 2 Timothy: A Commentary*. The New Testament Library. Edited by C. Clifton Black et al. Louisville: Westminster John Knox, 2012.

Congdon, David W. *Rudolf Bultmann: A Companion to His Theology*. Eugene, OR: Cascade, 2015.

Conzelmann, Hans. *An Outline of the Theology of the New Testament*. London: SCM, 1969.

Criswell, W. A. *Why I Preach That the Bible Is Literally True*. Edited by Timothy George and Denise George. Nashville: B&H, 1995.

Dabney, R. L. *Evangelical Eloquence: A Course of Lectures on Preaching*. Carlisle, PA: Banner of Truth Trust, 1999.

Dargan, Edwin C. *From the Apostolic Fathers to the Great Reformers A. D. 70–1572*. Vol. 1 of *A History of Preaching*. New York: Hodder & Stoughton, 1905.

Davis, Henry Grady. *Design for Preaching*. Minneapolis: Augsburg Fortress, 1958.

Dever, Mark. *The Church: The Gospel Made Visible*. Nashville: B&H Academic, 2012.

Dever, Mark, and Greg Gilbert. *Preach: Theology Meets Practice*. Nashville: B&H, 2012.

Dibelius, Martin. *From Tradition to Gospel*. 2nd ed. Translated by Bertram Lee Woolf. New York: Scribner, 1935.

Dodd, C. H. *The Apostolic Preaching and Its Developments*. New York: Harper & Brothers, 1962.

Drummond, Lewis A. "Build a Foundation for Effective Evangelistic Preaching." Preaching.com. https://www.preaching.com/articles/build-a-foundation-for-effective-evangelistic-preaching/.

———. *Reaching Generation Next: Effective Evangelism in Today's Culture*. Grand Rapids: Baker, 2002.

———. *The Word of the Cross: A Contemporary Theology of Evangelism*. Nashville: Broadman, 1992.

Dunn, James D. G. *Romans 1–8*. Word Biblical Commentary 38A. Edited by Bruce M. Metzger et al. Dallas: Word, 1988.

Elwell, Walter A., ed. *The Evangelical Dictionary of Biblical Theology*. Grand Rapids: Baker Academic, 1996.

Fee, Gordon, and Douglas Stuart. *How to Read the Bible for All Its Worth*. 4th ed. Grand Rapids: Zondervan Academic, 2014.

Gallaty, Robby, and Steven Smith. *Preaching for the Rest of Us: Essentials for Text-Driven Preaching*. Nashville: B&H Academic, 2018.

Garrett, Duane A. *Hosea, Joel*. New American Commentary 19A. Edited by E. Ray Clendenen. Nashville: Broadman & Holman, 1997.

Gibson, Scott M., and Matthew D. Kim, eds. *Homiletics and Hermeneutics: Four Views on Preaching Today*. Grand Rapids: Baker Academic, 2018.

Gilbert, Greg. *What Is the Gospel?* Wheaton, IL: Crossway, 2010.

Goldsworthy, Graeme. *Preaching the Whole Bible as Christian Scripture: The Application of Biblical Theology to Expository Preaching*. Grand Rapids: Eerdmans, 2000.

Green, Joel B. *The Gospel of Luke*. The New International Commentary on the New Testament. Grand Rapids: Eerdmans, 1977.

Green, Michael. *Evangelism in the Early Church*. Rev. ed. Grand Rapids: Eerdmans, 2003.

Griffiths, Jonathan L. *Preaching in the New Testament: An Exegetical and Biblical-Theological Study*. New Studies in Biblical Theology. Edited by D. A. Carson. Downers Grove, IL: InterVarsity, 2017.

Harris, Murray J. *The Second Epistle to the Corinthians*. New International Greek Testament Commentary. Edited by I. Howard Marshall and Donald A. Hagner. Grand Rapids: Eerdmans, 2005.

Hawkins, O. S., and Matt Queen. *The Gospel Invitation: Why Publicly Inviting People to Receive Christ Still Matters*. Nashville: Nelson, 2023.

Heckert, Jakob K. *Discourse Function of Conjoiners in the Pastoral Epistles*. Dallas: SIL International, 1991.

Helm, David. *Expositional Preaching: How We Speak God's Word Today*. Wheaton, IL: Crossway, 2014.

Hervey, A. C. *II Timothy*. The Pulpit Commentary 21. Edited by H. D. M. Spence. Grand Rapids: Eerdmans, 1958.

Hinson, E. Glenn. *The Evangelization of the Roman Empire: Identity and Adaptability*. Macon, GA: Mercer University Press, 1981.

Hughes, R. Kent, and Bryan Chapell. *1 & 2 Timothy and Titus: To Guard the Deposit*. Preaching the Word. Wheaton, IL: Crossway, 2000.

John Chrysostom. *Homilies of St. John Chrysostom, Archbishop of Constantinople, on the Second Epistle of St. Paul the Apostle to Timothy*. In *A Select Library of the Nicene and Post-Nicene Fathers*, 1st ser., edited by Philip Schaff, 13:475–518. New York: Christian Literature Company, 1889.

Kelley, Charles S. *Fuel the Fire: Lessons from the History of Southern Baptist Evangelism*. Nashville: B&H Academic, 2018.

———. *How Did They Do It? The Story of Southern Baptist Evangelism*. Chicago: Insight, 1993.

Kelly, J. N. D. *The Pastoral Epistles: 1 Timothy, 2 Timothy, and Titus*. Black's New Testament Commentary. Grand Rapids: A&C Black, 1986.

Kennedy, George A. *Classical Rhetoric and Its Christian and Secular Tradition from Ancient to Modern Times*. 2nd ed. Chapel Hill: University of North Carolina Press, 1999.

Kittel, Gerhard, et al., eds. *Theological Dictionary of the New Testament*. Electronic ed. Grand Rapids: Eerdmans, 1964. Logos Bible Software.

Knight, George W., III. *The Pastoral Epistles*. New International Greek Testament Commentary. Grand Rapids: Eerdmans, 1992.

Köstenberger, Andreas J., and Terry L. Wilder, eds. *Entrusted with the Gospel: Paul's Theology in the Pastoral Epistles*. Nashville: B&H Academic, 2010.

Kruse, Colin G. *Paul's Letter to the Romans*. The Pillar New Testament Commentary. Edited by D. A. Carson. Grand Rapids: Eerdmans, 2012.

Kuruvilla, Abraham. *Privilege the Text! A Theological Hermeneutic for Preaching*. Chicago: Moody, 2013.

Lange, Johann Peter, and F. R. Fay. *The Epistle of Paul to the Romans: A Commentary on the Holy Scriptures*. Translated by J. F. Hurst. Bellingham, WA: Logos Bible Software, 2008.

Lange, Johann Peter, and J. J. van Oosterzee. *A Commentary on the Holy Scriptures: Luke*. Translated by Philip Schaff and Charles C. Starbuck. Bellingham, WA: Logos Bible Software, 2008.

Larsen, David L. *The Company of Preachers: A History of Biblical Preaching from the Old Testament to the Modern Era*. 2 vols. Grand Rapids: Kregel Academic, 1998.

———. *The Evangelism Mandate: Recovering the Centrality of Gospel Preaching*. Grand Rapids: Kregel, 1992.

Lea, Thomas D., and Hayne P. Griffin. *1 Timothy, 2 Timothy, and Titus*. New American Commentary 34. Edited by David S. Dockery. Nashville: B&H, 1992.

Lenski, R. H. C. *The Interpretation of St. Paul's Epistles to the Colossians, to the Thessalonians, to Timothy, to Titus, and to Philemon*. Minneapolis: Augsburg, 1937.

Lischer, Richard, ed. *The Company of Preachers: Wisdom on Preaching, Augustine to the Present*. Grand Rapids: Eerdmans, 2002.

———. *Theology of Preaching: The Dynamics of the Gospel*. Rev. ed. Eugene, OR: Wipf and Stock, 1992.

Lloyd-Jones, D. Martyn. *Preaching and Preachers*. 40th anniv. ed. Grand Rapids: Zondervan, 2011.

Longenecker, Richard. *Biblical Exegesis in the Apostolic Period*. 2nd ed. Grand Rapids: Eerdmans, 1999.

Marshall, I. Howard. *The Gospel of Luke*. New International Greek Testament Commentary. Grand Rapids: Eerdmans, 1978.

Martin, D. Michael. *1, 2 Thessalonians*. New American Commentary 33. Edited by E. Ray Clendenen. Nashville: Broadman & Holman, 1995.

McCroskey, James C. *An Introduction to Rhetorical Communication*. 8th ed. Needham, MA: Prentice-Hall, 2001.

McKellar, Matthew F. "An Evaluation of the Elements of Persuasion in the Favorite Messages of W. A. Criswell as Contained in the Book 'With a Bible in My Hand.'" PhD diss., Southwestern Baptist Theological Seminary, 1991.

McKnight, Scot. *King Jesus Gospel: The Original Good News Revisited*. Rev. ed. Grand Rapids: Zondervan, 2011.

Merida, Tony. *Faithful Preaching: Declaring Scripture with Responsibility, Passion, and Authenticity*. Nashville: B&H, 2009.

Merrill, Eugene H. *Deuteronomy*. New American Commentary 4. Edited by E. Ray Clendenen. Nashville: Broadman & Holman, 1994.

Meyer, Jason C. *Preaching: A Biblical Theology of Preaching*. Wheaton, IL: Crossway, 2013.

Moo, Douglas J. *The Letter to the Romans*. 2nd ed. The New International Commentary of the New Testament. Edited by Joel B. Green. Grand Rapids: Eerdmans, 2018.

Morris, Leon. *The Epistle to the Romans*. The Pillar New Testament Commentary. Edited by D. A. Carson. Grand Rapids: Eerdmans, 1988.

Mounce, Robert H. *The Essential Nature of New Testament Preaching*. Eugene, OR: Wipf and Stock, 1960.

———. *Romans*. New American Commentary 27. Edited by E. Ray Clendenen. Nashville: Broadman & Holman, 1995.

Mounce, William D. *Pastoral Epistles*. Word Biblical Commentary 46. Edited by Bruce M. Metzger et al. Grand Rapids: Zondervan, 2000.

Newman, Barclay M., and Eugene A. Nida. *A Translator's Handbook on Paul's Letter to the Romans*. New York: United Bible Societies, 1973.

———. *A Translator's Handbook on the Acts of the Apostles*. New York: United Bible Society, 1972.

Newman, Randy. *Mere Evangelism: 10 Insights from C. S. Lewis to Help You Share Your Faith*. Epsom, UK: The Good Book Company, 2021.

Osborne, Grant R. *1 & 2 Thessalonians: Verse by Verse*. Osborne New Testament Commentaries. Edited by Elliot Ritzema et al. Bellingham, WA: Lexham, 2018.

———. *Acts: Verse by Verse*. Osborne New Testament Commentaries. Edited by Elliot Ritzema et al. Bellingham, WA: Lexham, 2019.

———. *Hermeneutical Spiral: A Comprehensive Introduction to Biblical Interpretation*. Rev. and expanded. Downers Grove, IL: IVP Academic, 2006.

———. *Luke: Verse by Verse*. Osborne New Testament Commentaries. Edited by Elliot Ritzema et al. Bellingham, WA: Lexham, 2018.

———. *Romans: Verse by Verse*. Osborne New Testament Commentaries. Edited by Elliot Ritzema et al. Bellingham, WA: Lexham, 2017.

Owen, John. *The Glory of Christ*. Edited by R. J. K. Law. Carlisle, PA: Banner of Truth Trust, 1994.

Perkins, William. *The Art of Prophesying and the Calling of the Ministry*. Carlisle, PA: Banner of Truth Trust, 1996.

Perry, Lloyd M., and John R. Strubhar. *Evangelistic Preaching*. Eugene, OR: Wipf and Stock, 2000.

Péter-Contesse, René, and John Ellington. *A Handbook on Leviticus*. United Bible Society Handbook Series. New York: United Bible Societies, 1992.

Peterson, David G. *The Acts of the Apostles*. The Pillar New Testament Commentary. Edited by D. A. Carson. Grand Rapids: Eerdmans, 2009.

Piper, John. *The Supremacy of God in Preaching*. Grand Rapids: Baker, 2015.

Plummer, Robert L. *Paul's Understanding of the Church's Mission: Did the Apostle Paul Expect the Early Christian Communities to Evangelize?* Waynesboro, GA: Paternoster, 2006.

Poe, Harry L. *The Gospel and Its Meaning: A Theology for Evangelism and Church Growth*. Grand Rapids: Zondervan, 1996.

Polhill, John B. *Acts*. New American Commentary 26. Edited by E. Ray Clendenen. Nashville: Broadman & Holman, 1992.

Price, Wm. Craig, ed. *Engage: Tools for Contemporary Evangelism*. Birmingham, AL: Iron Stream Media, 2019.

Queen, Matt. *Recapturing Evangelism: A Biblical-Theological Approach*. Nashville: B&H Academic, 2023.

———. "A Theological Assessment of the Gospel Content in Selected Southern Baptist Sources." PhD diss., Southeastern Baptist Theological Seminary, 2009.

Reiling, J., and J. L. Swellengrebel. *A Handbook on the Gospel of Luke*. UBS Handbook Series. New York: United Bible Societies, 1993.

Richards, I. A. *The Philosophy of Rhetoric*. London: Oxford University Press, 1936.

Robinson, Haddon W. *On Biblical Preaching: The Development and Delivery of Expository Messages*. 3rd ed. Grand Rapids: Baker Academic, 2014.

Robinson, Haddon W., and Craig B. Larson, eds. *The Art and Craft of Biblical Preaching: A Comprehensive Resource for Today's Communicators*. Grand Rapids: Zondervan Academic, 2005.

Rogers, Adrian P. *Preaching for Impact*. Memphis, TN: Love Worth Finding Ministries, 2021.

Rooker, Mark F. *Leviticus*. New American Commentary 3A. Edited by E. Ray Clendenen. Nashville: Broadman & Holman, 2000.

Ryle, J. C. *Luke*. Expository Thoughts on the Gospels 2. Grand Rapids: Baker, 1990.

Schnabel, Eckhard J. *Paul the Missionary: Realities, Strategies, and Methods*. Downers Grove, IL: InterVarsity, 2008.

Sertillanges, A. G. *The Intellectual Life: Its Spirits, Conditions, and Methods*. Translated by Mary Ryan. Washington, DC: Catholic University of America Press, 1987.

Shakespeare, William. *The Complete Signet Classic Shakespeare*. Edited by Sylvan Barnet. New York: Harcourt Brace Jovanovich, 1963.

Simeon, Charles. *2 Timothy to Hebrews*. Vol. 19 of *Horae Homileticae*. London: Holdsworth & Ball, 1833.

———. *Genesis to Leviticus*. Vol. 1 of *Horae Homileticae*. London: Holdsworth, 1863.

———. *Romans*. Vol. 15 of *Horae Homileticae*. London: Holdsworth & Ball, 1883.

Smith, Gary V. *Isaiah 40–66*. New American Commentary 15B. Edited by E. Ray Clendenen. Nashville: Broadman & Holman, 2009.

Smith, J. Josh. *Preaching for a Verdict: Recovering the Role of Exhortation*. Nashville: B&H Academic, 2019.

Smith, Steven W. *Dying to Preach: Embracing the Cross in the Pulpit*. Grand Rapids: Kregel, 2009.

———. "The Essential Elements of Text-Driven Preaching." Equip the Called, Sept. 1, 2016. https://equipthecalled.com/ps-article/the-essential-elements-of-text-driven-preaching/.

———. *Recapturing the Voice of God: Shaping Sermons Like Scripture*. Nashville: B&H, 2015.

Soards, Marion L. *The Speeches in Acts: Their Content, Context, and Concerns*. Louisville: Westminster/John Knox, 1994.

Spence, H. D. M. *The Gospel According to Luke*. The Pulpit Commentary 16. Grand Rapids: Eerdmans, 1953.

Spurgeon, Charles H. *Lectures to My Students*. 4 vols. Las Vegas, NV: Dream International, 2021.

———. *The New Park Street Pulpit*. 5 vols. London: Passmore & Alabaster, 1860.

———. *The Soul Winner: How to Lead Sinners to the Savior*. San Bernardino, CA: Legacy, 2016.

Stein, Robert H. *Luke*. New American Commentary 24. Edited by David S. Dockery. Nashville: B&H, 1992.

Stewart, James S. *A Faith to Proclaim*. New York: Scribner's Sons, 1953.

———. *Heralds of God: The Warrack Lectures*. London: Hodder & Stoughton, 1961.

Stott, John R. W. *Between Two Worlds: The Challenge of Preaching Today*. Grand Rapids: Eerdmans, 1982.

———. *God's Word for Today's World*. Cumbria, UK: Langham Preaching Resources, 2015.

Strain, David. *Expositional Preaching*. Phillipsburg, NJ: P&R, 2021.

Streett, R. Alan. *The Effective Invitation: A Practical Guide for the Pastor*. Grand Rapids: Kregel, 1984.

Thompson, James A. *Apostle of Persuasion: Theology and Rhetoric in the Pauline Letters*. Grand Rapids: Baker Academic, 2020.

Tripp, Paul David. *War of Words: Getting to the Heart of Your Communication Struggle*. Phillipsburg, NJ: P&R, 2000.

Walker, C. Kyle. *Let the Text Talk: Preaching That Treats the Text on Its Own Terms*. Fort Worth, TX: Seminary Hill, 2018.

Washer, Paul. *The Preeminent Christ: God's Beautiful and Unchanging Gospel*. Grand Rapids: Reformation Heritage, 2023.

Wilkens, Steve, ed. *Christian Ethics: Four Views*. Downers Grove, IL: IVP Academic, 2017.

Witherington, Ben, III. *The Acts of the Apostles: A Socio-Rhetorical Commentary*. Grand Rapids: Eerdmans, 1998.

Wright, N. T. *How God Became King: The Forgotten Story of the Gospels*. San Francisco: HarperOne, 2016.

York, Hershael W., and Bert Decker. *Preaching with Bold Assurance: A Solid and Enduring Approach to Engaging Exposition*. Nashville: B&H, 2003.

www.ingramcontent.com/pod-product-compliance
Lightning Source LLC
LaVergne TN
LVHW050646100826
845148LV00011B/2007

* 9 7 9 8 3 8 5 2 6 6 8 5 2 *